Barefoot in Paris

BAREFOOT IN PARIS

Ina Garten

PHOTOGRAPHS BY QUENTIN BACON

BANTAM PRESS

LONDON · NEW YORK · TORONTO · SYDNEY · AUCKLAND

TRANSWORLD PUBLISHERS
61–63 Uxbridge Road, London W5 5SA
A Random House Group Company
www.transworldbooks.co.uk

First published in the United States by Clarkson Potter/Publishers, New York,
member of the Crown Publishing Group,
a division of Random House, Inc.

First published in Great Britain
in 2012 by Bantam Press
an imprint of Transworld Publishers

Design by Marysarah Quinn

ISBN 9780593068434

Printed and bound in China

2 4 6 8 10 9 7 5 3 1

CONVERSION CHART

Oven Temperatures:
130°C = 250°F = Gas mark ½
150°C = 300°F = Gas mark 2
180°C = 350°F = Gas mark 4
190°C = 375°F = Gas mark 5
200°C = 400°F = Gas mark 6
220°C = 425°F = Gas mark 7
230°C = 450°F = Gas mark 8

Spoon Measures:
1 level tablespoon flour = 15g
1 heaped tablespoon flour = 28g
1 level tablespoon sugar = 28g
1 level tablespoon butter = 15g

American Solid Measures:
1 cup rice US = 225g
1 cup flour US = 115g
1 cup butter US = 225g
1 stick butter US = 115g
1 cup dried fruit US = 225g
1 cup brown sugar US = 180g
1 cup granulated sugar US = 225g

Liquid Measures:
1 cup US = 275ml
1 pint US = 550ml
1 quart US = 900ml

For Jeffrey,
who makes Paris
so *delicious*

Thanks

First, I want to thank my wonderful friend and assistant, Barbara Libath, who works side by side with me every day. After I wrote and tested each recipe in this book, Barbara retested them again to make sure they really worked. The look on her face when she took a blue cheese soufflé or lemon meringue tart out of the oven has kept me motivated for the entire year. I can't imagine doing this without her.

So many other people keep me going. My extraordinary and supportive editor, Pam Krauss, and my family at Clarkson Potter/Publishers, including Jenny Frost, Lauren Shakely, and Marysarah Quinn, all make me feel—against all reason—as though I know what I'm doing. Thank you, especially, Marysarah, for your beautiful book design. My wonderful agent, Esther Newberg at ICM, is brilliant at the business side of books and lets me focus on the fun stuff: the writing.

Thank you to the endlessly creative team of people who helped me make this book: Quentin Bacon for the gorgeous photographs; Rori Trovato, who makes the food look so delicious—and has such a good time doing it; and Miguel Flores-Vianna, who brings such style to all our shoots. I love you all dearly and I'm so grateful that you make it all so joyous.

I also want to thank the people who have developed my interest in French food. To Julia Child, who taught us all. We've never met, but your books gave me, and a whole generation of cooks, a foundation for cooking real French food. Thank you also to Anna Pump of Loaves and Fishes in Sagaponack, New York; Patricia Wells, author of *The Food Lover's Guide to Paris* and lots of wonderful French cookbooks; and Lydie Marshall. You've all inspired me.

But most of all, thank you to my sweet husband, Jeffrey, who encourages me to do what's fun first and who takes me to Paris and shows me the time of my life.

Contents

Introduction

It all started with a dress. When I was three years old, my grandparents went to Paris and brought me back a ruffly, off-the-shoulders party dress that we called my Paris dress. I felt really pretty in it. I didn't know where Paris was, but I knew I couldn't wait to go there.

When we were first married, my husband, Jeffrey, took me to Europe for the first time on an American Express tour: three cities, six nights! I'd dreamed of going to Paris for so long and it was, as every first-time visitor finds out, even better than expected. I think there might have even been a few tears. Paris is really a woman's city—gorgeous people, elegant restaurants, wide boulevards with allées of trees, beautiful gardens and parks. What I couldn't get over, though, were the street markets: every day in different parts of the city, farmers and food purveyors would set up stalls and sell their incredibly delicious produce, farmhouse cheeses, and homemade baked goods. I couldn't wait to go home and start cooking French food.

A few years after that, Jeffrey and I went back to France, this time for a four-month camping trip. With our little Renault 4, a Day-Glo orange tent, sleeping bags, and a map of the campgrounds, we traveled all over France. It sounds impossible now, but we had a budget of five dollars a day and we lived really well. For breakfast I'd go off to a local bakery and buy croissants and crusty French rolls hot out of the oven. For lunch, we'd hit the market and collect slices of pâté, wedges of fragrant Brie, and some fresh peaches. I can still taste how good they were. We'd find a bench in a gorgeous little park and we'd eat our lunch. For dinner, I'd set up a little gas stove near our tiny tent and I'd cook dinner or heat up some cassoulet or beef bour-

Shopping in the market on Boulevard Raspail.

guignon from a local charcuterie. I'll never forget pulling into one campsite in Normandy. The owner of the site offered to bring us some coq au vin, chicken cooked in wine, that she'd made for her husband that night. Now I *really* wanted to go home and cook French food!

And that's exactly what I did. After the camping trip, we moved to Washington, D.C., where we were both working for the government. Food, however, was becoming my passion. I bought Julia Child's *Mastering the Art of French Cooking*, volumes one and two, and for the next seven years, I cooked my way through those wonderful books. I'd work on the President's nuclear energy policy all day and I'd rush home and cook all night. It was the best cooking education I could have had. I held a dinner party almost every weekend and all week long I'd spend my evenings preparing for it. How crazy was that?

By 1978, after years of working in the White House, I was ready to take a chance in the food business. I bought Barefoot Contessa, then a small specialty food store in the Hamptons. I really didn't have a clue what I was doing, I just used my experience cooking for friends to teach myself how to cook for customers in the store. The beef bourguignon and raspberry tarts that I sold in the store were the same as the ones I would make for six friends on Saturday night. Now, though, I had to learn to keep a recipe really easy because I needed to cook a hundred quarts of beef bourguignon and two hundred raspberry tarts!

I wanted to understand more about French food, so I signed up for cooking classes with Lydie Marshall, a wonderful teacher who grew up in Provence and had a school in her townhouse in Greenwich Village, near where I lived in the off-season. About twelve students would show up each evening. We'd get assignments for the meal—the beginners made the salad and the experts cooked the main course—and we'd cook away the

evenings. Lydie taught *country* French food—dinners such as coq au vin with potato and celery root purée, and for dessert, a rustic lemon tart and *île flottante,* or floating island. Those were some of the most wonderful evenings I ever spent and they really influenced how I think about food. Lydie used good, simple ingredients and looked for the synergy between them: veal with morels, pears and blue cheese, peaches and Sauternes. Most of all, from Lydie I learned to respect the essence of the ingredients. If the raspberries were in season, she didn't do much to make them taste better; she cooked to enhance that essential "raspberriness" of the fruit, not to overpower it.

Americans think of French food as fancy food. We think of French restaurants as formal places where we're always about to commit some hideous breach of etiquette. We think of French food as special-occasion food. It's true that some French food is elaborate and formal, but there are so many kinds of French food. What I love is simple, country French food, and I wanted to cook it in a way that was easy enough for me to use not only at Barefoot Contessa but also for entertaining at home. So, that's what I did. When I wrote my books, I included many of the French recipes that I'd developed over the years. In *The Barefoot Contessa Cookbook* there's a recipe for beef bourguignon my way. Instead of the usual stew that cooks for hours, I prepared it with a filet of beef so it's not only more delicious but also much quicker to make. In *Barefoot Contessa Parties!*, there's a plum tart, but the crust is made of shortbread, so you press it into the pan rather than wrestling with a traditional pastry crust. Other dishes, such as the Provençal tomatoes in *Barefoot Contessa Family Style*, are so simple and delicious that they don't really need a twist—they're wonderful just as they are.

I also like a recipe I can use over and over again. I love cassoulet and bouillabaisse, but I've discovered that they really *do* take all day to make, so I order them when I go out to a French restaurant. Other dishes like blue cheese soufflé are so easy that they are worth mastering. And I have to say, nothing gets a bigger *Wow!* from my friends than pulling that soufflé out of the oven. Chicken with morels is really easy to cook but it's elegant enough for a special dinner, and the best part is it can be made in advance, so it's great for a dinner party. French cooking can be even simpler: Wouldn't your friends be delighted if you served them big bowls of steaming coffee with hot milk for breakfast and toasted baguettes slathered with butter and honey? I would! For dinner, forget all those fancy sauces that either take hours to prepare or have to be made at the last minute when everyone's hungry for dinner. In this book you'll find plenty of traditional recipes, such as scallops Provençal and chicken with forty cloves of garlic, for which the sauce actually happens in the cooking. And then there's dessert. If you don't even have ten minutes to make the crème brûlée or coeur à la crème (and I do mean ten minutes!), just remember how French it is to serve a big bowl of fresh strawberries in season with just a dollop of crème fraîche and a cookie from the bakery.

It's hard to believe my life-long interest in French cooking all started with a dress, and it's not over yet. All my life I dreamed of an apartment in Paris where I could cook, and now I have one, on the Left Bank. It has bright orange awnings, views of the rooftops across the city, and a big park filled with plane trees just under my windows. Of course, I just had to have that French stove of my dreams, too—a big La Cornue that six men had to carry up five flights of winding stairs. But to tell you the truth, that stove hasn't changed the way I cook. It's a short walk from my apartment to all my favorite places: Poilâne for crusty breads, Barthélémy for really ripe cheeses, a wonderful street market for organic produce, and La Grande Epicerie, a huge specialty food store, for everything else. When I turn on my fancy stove it's usually just to roast the same kind of chicken that I make in East Hampton. Instead of a chicken from Iacono Farm, it's a *poulet de Bresse*, but it's really the same thing. There's nothing in this book that I make in that fancy oven that you can't make in your own kitchen at home. I hope you'll find lots of entertaining ideas here and recipes that will not only wow your family and friends, but also convince you how easy it is to cook really delicious French food, even if it's not a special occasion.

My brother Ken with me in my Paris dress.

to start

Raspberry Royale

Kir

Cassis à l'Eau

Cheese Straws

Blini with Smoked Salmon

Cheese Puffs

Rosemary Cashews

Radishes with Butter and Salt

Potato Chips

About French Wine

It's really hard to know about wine. Every time I pick up a book determined to learn something about the subject, I get mired in the details of grapes and tannin and vintages, when all I really want to know is, "What would be good to serve with this rack of lamb?" When we first moved to New York City in 1978, my husband took me to Lutèce, the best French restaurant in the city, for my birthday. I was handed a wine list with pages and pages of options and had not the slightest idea of how to choose. When I finally ordered one of the three bottles that was under a hundred dollars, I had to admit to Jeffrey that I wasn't even sure if it was a red or a white wine!

Recently, I decided to ask an expert to help me sort out at least the basics of French wines. This overview is definitely *not* for an expert (if you know a lot about wine, don't e-mail me!). It's for someone like me who wants to walk into a wine store and ask for something to drink with dinner without feeling like a total idiot. So, here goes.

Unlike American wines, which are classified by the predominant grape used, such as Chardonnay or Pinot Noir, French wines are classified by the region in which they're grown, such as Champagne, Bordeaux, or Burgundy. Of course, what a wine tastes like has an enormous amount to do with the type of grape, the quality of the soil, the weather, and the winemaking process.

I have two broad guidelines for thinking about choosing a wine. First, I think about the wine the way I think about a sauce: I want something that will complement the dish rather than compete with it. I wouldn't put a strong, spicy green peppercorn sauce on a delicate fillet of sole any more than I'd serve it with a big, spicy red wine. Here is where a crisp, fruity white wine such as Sancerre from the Loire would be delicious. The second guideline I use is the French saying "What grows together, goes together." So, when I'm making an earthy Provençal dish such as pissaladière (an onion pizza with olives and anchovies), I might choose a rustic Provençal red wine, such as Bandol, to go with it. There are many French wine regions, but here is an overview of the five that are best known.

Everyone's favorite region is Champagne, whose sparkling wines are named for the châteaux that produce them. We know so many of those elegant names: Veuve Clicquot, Moët et Chandon, Dom Pérignon. As with other wines, whether you end up with a white or red wine relies not on the color of grape but rather on whether the skins are used in the production. Therefore, Champagne can come from a white Chardonnay grape or a red Pinot Noir grape and you still end up with a white sparkling wine. Rosé Champagne is generally made by adding a bit of still red wine before adding the bubbles. Champagne goes with almost anything, from appetizers to dinner to cheese and on through dessert. The Champagne classification *brut* literally means "dry," and it refers to the sweetness of the wine. The better Champagnes are almost all brut, but the more expensive the Champagne, the more complex the flavor. A very special Champagne such as Veuve Clicquot La Grande Dame may be brut but it's also full of flavor, and, when I pour some for a celebration, I feel that life doesn't get any better than this.

Bordeaux is the next best-known winemaking area and its wines are classified by subregion, such as Pomerol and Saint-Emilion. As with Champagnes, though, they are more likely to be named after the château where they're produced, such as Château Margaux and Château Mouton-Rothschild, than for the region. Bordeaux are full-bodied. The red wines, predominantly from Cabernet and Merlot grapes, have a rich red color, and the flavor is usually characterized by spicy fruit tones such as black currant, plum, spice, and cassis. When they're young, they can be astringent, but as they age, they develop round, complex, fruity flavors. The foods associated with the region ("what grows together, goes together")—lamb and duck—are particularly good with Bordeaux wines.

Burgundy wines are produced by lots of small estates that combine their grapes to make one wine, and they're often named for the local region, such as Beaune, Pommard, and Chablis, rather than for a single château. Some bottles are labeled with the name of the region and the name of the importer, such as Louis Jadot and Louis Latour. Red Burgundies, made from the Pinot Noir grape, tend to be lighter in color than Bordeaux but that certainly doesn't mean they have less flavor. These wines are generally characterized by fragrant red fruit tones such as raspberry, blackberry, cherry, and currant and sometimes also woodsy mushroom flavors. The red wines of Burgundy are delicious with their local beef and rabbit. White Burgundies are made from

Chardonnay grapes, but they range from light and dry, such as a Macon, to really big and full of flavor—with tones of honey and nuts—such as Meursault and Chassagne-Montrachet. These white wines are delicious with chicken and seafood, which are popular in Burgundy.

Loire Valley white wines are made predominantly from the Sauvignon Blanc grapes and can range from a Pouilly-Fumé, which is oaky and dry, to a Sancerre, a light, crisp, dry white that goes very well with the pork and goat cheese that are found in the region.

Finally, Rhône wines come from an area in the south that is sunny and hot, and the wines reflect the region. Both the red and white wines are full and robust and often not very expensive, such as Gigondas. One of my favorite wines, white Châteauneuf-du-Pape, comes from this region. It's full of buttery flavor without the acidity that's sometimes associated with a young white wine.

But at the end of the day, the only thing that counts is what you like. The old rules of white wine with fish and chicken and red wine with meat have been discarded in favor of drinking anything that tastes good to you. It's always smart to find a good retailer and build a relationship with him or her. Ask for recommendations to go with the particular dish you'll be serving; it's their job to know which wines complement different foods.

For me, the best way to learn about wine is to buy several different wines in one category, such as Burgundy, and serve them all together at a party. Everyone has fun tasting the wines, bottles are passed back and forth, we laugh about the descriptions everyone comes up with, and maybe, if we're lucky, we might even learn something. How bad can that be?

The old rules of white wine with fish and red wine with meat have been discarded in favor of drinking anything that tastes good to you.

Raspberry Royale

Kir royale is Champagne with a splash of crème de cassis. I decided to try it with raspberry liqueur and it was even more delicious. When you go to the liquor store, look for the red raspberry liqueur rather than the clear eau-de-vie, which has a totally different flavor.

> 6 teaspoons raspberry liqueur
> ½ pint fresh raspberries
> 1 bottle of good Champagne, chilled

Pour 1 teaspoon of raspberry liqueur into each champagne glass and add 2 or 3 raspberries. When guests arrive, pop the cork and fill each glass with Champagne. Serve immediately.

Kir

A kir is an apértif of white wine with a splash of crème de cassis. The cassis adds a hint of fruit and a lovely tinge of pink but it's not too sweet. I prefer to make them with a crisp, fruity wine, such as Sauvignon Blanc from California or Sancerre from France, but whatever you have on hand is fine.

6 teaspoons crème de cassis liqueur
1 bottle white wine, chilled

Pour 1 to 2 teaspoons of crème de cassis into each wine glass and then fill the glass with wine. Serve chilled.

Cassis à l'Eau

MAKES 1 DRINK

The French serve cassis mixed with water for a low-alcohol twist on a kir. It's very refreshing on a hot summer day.

6 tablespoons crème de cassis liqueur
¾ cup water

Fill a tumbler with ice. Pour in the cassis and water and stir.

Cheese Straws

MAKES 22 TO 24 STRAWS

In Paris, I was lucky to be invited to dinner at the house once lived in by Louis Vuitton, which is now an amazing museum filled with his old suitcases dating back to the mid-nineteenth century. With cocktails, the hosts served only freshly baked cheese straws piled high, Lincoln Log–style, on a square platter. They're meant to stimulate your appetite for dinner, not to ruin it. With frozen puff pastry from the grocery store, these cheese straws are really easy to make.

> 2 sheets (1 box) frozen puff pastry (such as Pepperidge Farm), defrosted overnight in the refrigerator
> 1 extra-large egg
> ½ cup freshly grated Parmesan cheese
> 1 cup finely grated Gruyère cheese
> 1 teaspoon minced fresh thyme leaves
> 1 teaspoon kosher salt
> Freshly ground black pepper

Preheat the oven to 375 degrees.

You want to work quickly because the puff pastry needs to stay cold until it's baked.

Roll out each sheet of puff pastry on a lightly floured board until it's 10 × 12 inches. Beat the egg with 1 tablespoon of water and brush the surface of the pastry. Sprinkle each sheet evenly with ¼ cup of the Parmesan, ½ cup of the Gruyère, ½ teaspoon of the thyme, ½ teaspoon of the salt, and some pepper. With the rolling pin, lightly press the flavorings into the puff pastry. Cut each sheet crosswise with a floured knife or pizza wheel into 11 or 12 strips. Twist each strip and lay on baking sheets lined with parchment paper.

Bake for 10 to 15 minutes, until lightly browned and puffed. Turn each straw and bake for another 2 minutes. Don't overbake or the cheese will burn. Cool and serve at room temperature.

You can also
brush the pastry
with pesto,
tapenade, or sun-
dried tomato
paste instead of
sprinkling with
the cheeses.

Blini with Smoked Salmon

MAKES 18 TO 20 PANCAKES

I wrote this recipe for an article on entertaining in Martha Stewart Living *magazine. Blini are little buckwheat pancakes that you can top with smoked salmon, caviar, and/or a dollop of crème fraîche. I make the batter early, but since they're best served warm, I prefer to cook them after guests arrive. Everyone's invited into the kitchen for drinks, and while I cook the blini, one of the guests assembles the toppings and serves them.*

⅓ cup buckwheat flour
⅔ cup all-purpose flour
½ teaspoon baking powder
¾ teaspoon kosher salt
¾ cup plus 2 tablespoons milk
1 extra-large egg
¼ pound (1 stick) unsalted butter, clarified (see Note)
½ pound smoked salmon, thinly sliced
¼ cup crème fraîche or sour cream
Fresh dill, for garnish

Combine the two flours, baking powder, and salt in a bowl. In a separate bowl, whisk together the milk, egg, and 1 tablespoon of the clarified butter, then whisk into the flour mixture. Heat 1 tablespoon of the clarified butter in a medium sauté pan and drop the batter into the hot skillet, 1 tablespoon at a time. Cook over medium-low heat until bubbles form on the top side of the blini, about 2 minutes. Flip and cook for 1 more minute, or until brown. Repeat with the remaining batter. (I clean the hot pan with a dry paper towel between batches.) Set aside.

To serve, top the blini with a piece of smoked salmon. Add a dollop of crème fraîche and a sprig of dill.

To clarify the butter, melt it in a saucepan over low heat. Remove the white foam that comes to the surface, then allow the butter to sit at room temperature until the milk solids sink to the bottom. Pour off the golden liquid and discard the white sediment.

To make ahead, reheat the blini in a 300-degree oven for 5 to 10 minutes before assembling.

Cheese Puffs

GOUGÈRES

MAKES ABOUT 40 PUFFS

Pâte à choux dough seems complicated the first time you make it, but it really takes only a little bit of technique and you can use it for so many other things, such as cream puffs, profiteroles (page 219), and éclairs. Many restaurants in Paris bring you a little plate of hot gougères while you're waiting for dinner; I love to serve them with cocktails. You can make them in advance, freeze them, and then just heat and serve.

1 cup milk
¼ pound (1 stick) unsalted butter
1 teaspoon kosher salt
⅛ teaspoon freshly ground black pepper
Pinch of nutmeg
1 cup all-purpose flour
4 extra-large eggs
½ cup grated Gruyère cheese, plus extra for sprinkling
¼ cup freshly grated Parmesan cheese
1 egg beaten with 1 teaspoon water, for egg wash

Preheat the oven to 425 degrees. Line 2 baking sheets with parchment paper.

To scald milk, heat it to just below the boiling point.

In a saucepan, heat the milk, butter, salt, pepper, and nutmeg over medium heat, until scalded. Add the flour all at once and beat it vigorously with a wooden spoon until the mixture comes together. Cook, stirring constantly, over low heat for 2 minutes. The flour will begin to coat the bottom of the pan. Dump the hot mixture into the bowl of a food processor fitted with the steel blade. Immediately add the eggs, Gruyère, and Parmesan and pulse until the eggs are incorporated and the dough is smooth and thick.

Spoon the mixture into a pastry bag fitted with a large plain round tip. Pipe in mounds 1¼ inches wide and ¾ inch high onto the baking sheets. With a wet finger, lightly press down the swirl at the top of each puff. (You can also use two spoons to scoop out the mixture and shape the puffs with damp fingers.) Brush the top of each puff lightly with egg wash and sprinkle with a pinch of Gruyère. Bake for 15 minutes, or until golden brown outside but still soft inside.

To freeze, bake the puffs, allow them to cool, and freeze in a sealed plastic bag. Reheat at 425 degrees for 5 minutes.

Rosemary Cashews

SERVES 8

Here is another savory cocktail nibble that would satisfy a French host's needs. These cashews were inspired by the bar nuts served at Union Square Cafe in New York City, which is one of my favorite restaurants in the world. The cashews are best served warm but you can prepare the rosemary mixture in advance.

> 1 pound roasted unsalted cashews
> 2 tablespoons minced fresh rosemary leaves
> ½ teaspoon cayenne pepper
> 2 teaspoons light brown sugar
> 1 tablespoon kosher salt
> 1 tablespoon unsalted butter, melted

Preheat the oven to 350 degrees.

Spread the cashews out on a sheet pan. Toast in the oven until warm, about 5 minutes.

In a large bowl, combine the rosemary, cayenne, sugar, salt, and butter. Thoroughly toss the warm cashews with the spiced butter and serve warm.

Radishes with Butter and Salt

How simple is this? It is derived from a very old-fashioned French snack for children: a radish sandwiched between two slices of buttered bread. With drinks, I often serve plain or herbed butter spread on slices of French bread and a big bowl of radishes with sea salt.

> 2 bunches of radishes with the tops intact
> Sea salt
> Good salted butter or Herbed Butter (recipe follows)
> 1 French baguette, sliced diagonally, and lightly toasted

Arrange the radishes on a bed of sea salt. Spread the butter on slices of toasted bread and arrange artfully on a platter. Serve at room temperature.

HERBED BUTTER

> ¼ pound unsalted butter, at room temperature
> 1½ teaspoons minced scallions
> 1½ teaspoons minced fresh dill
> 1½ teaspoons minced fresh parsley
> ½ teaspoon freshly squeezed lemon juice
> ½ teaspoon kosher salt
> Pinch freshly ground black pepper

Combine all the ingredients in the bowl of an electric mixer fitted with the paddle attachment on low speed until combined. Do not whip.

Potato Chips

SERVES 6

I spent days frying potatoes in oil to find a chip that didn't have to be fried just before serving with drinks. Finally, I discovered that if I fried these potatoes early, I could reheat them on a baking sheet and they were even crisper and more flavorful than right out of the hot oil. They're also good with a steak for dinner!

    2 pounds Idaho potatoes, peeled
    Peanut or canola oil
    Sea salt or kosher salt

Slice the potatoes 1/16 inch thick with a vegetable slicer or mandoline. Soak the slices in cold water, drain the water, and soak one more time to eliminate some of the starch.

Meanwhile, place 2 to 3 inches of peanut oil in a large heavy-bottomed pot and heat it to 375 degrees on a candy thermometer. Drain the potatoes and pat them dry. Toss a handful of potatoes into the hot oil and fry them until they're golden brown, about 3 minutes, tossing to cook evenly. Be careful of the hot fat! Remove the potatoes with a slotted spoon or wire basket and drain on paper towels. Repeat the frying with the remaining potatoes.

Before serving, heat the oven to 350 degrees.

Place all the potatoes in a single layer on a baking sheet and bake for 5 minutes. Sprinkle generously with salt and serve.

lunch

Croque Monsieur

Blue Cheese Soufflé

Salad with Warm Goat Cheese

Eggplant Gratin

Pissaladière

Goat Cheese Tart

Scrambled Eggs with Truffles

Herbed-Baked Eggs

Spinach in Puff Pastry

Mussels in White Wine

Seafood Platter

About French Table Settings

What is it about French women that makes them so chic? A simple suit, the perfectly tied scarf—it not only looks great but they make a woman look gorgeous without being too studied, which is really the point. Coco Chanel said, "Dress shabbily and they notice the dress; dress impeccably and they notice the woman." Their secret is in finding one perfect style, one silhouette, and doing it over and over again in different colors and textures. A tailored gray wool suit with pants and a colorful Hermès scarf looks as elegant at the office as the same outfit in different materials—an unlined black velvet jacket with black satin pants and a white silk scarf—does for evening. Same silhouette, totally different look, perfectly accessorized.

Well, it turns out the same is true for table settings. I don't think any of my friends realize that for most of my dinner parties I do the same table setting over and over again, because the settings look totally different each time. Of course, my starting point for the setting is what makes the best party. A round table that's a little too small—everyone's seated elbow to elbow—creates just the right mood. Everyone can talk to everyone else and no one is left out of the conversation all the way at the end of a long table. The flowers in the middle are low so we can see each other and the candles are brighter than the room, which brings everyone's attention to the center of the table. But even with that structure, I still have to make the table look gorgeous, and I dress the table the way French women dress themselves: one silhouette, different materials, beautifully accessorized.

My starting point is usually the flowers. I go to Bridgehampton Florist to see what's in stock. If it's spring and they have white and lime-green flowers, I'll take my cue from those colors and set a table with a white cloth and beautiful green plates. If the table needs more "accessories," I'll add French water glasses with a green swirl in them and a wine glass to give the table height. If it's autumn and I find flowers that are orange and burgundy, the cloth might be a natural linen color with orange napkins and white plates. Once you have a system for designing a table, you'll find it's so much less stressful to pull everything together in the heat of organizing a dinner party, and your friends will never know how easy it was.

I dress the table the way French women dress themselves: one silhouette, different materials, beautifully accessorized.

Croque Monsieur

SERVES 4 TO 8

One day, my friend Frank Newbold and I found ourselves on the way to the Louvre at lunchtime. We passed Café Ruc, which is one of the Costes brothers' restaurants, and spotted two seats outside under the awning. They serve traditional French food, but with a modern twist. This was inspired by the delicious croque monsieurs we ate there. These sandwiches are on the small side, so serve one or two per person, depending on appetites.

2 tablespoons unsalted butter
3 tablespoons all-purpose flour
2 cups hot milk
1 teaspoon kosher salt
½ teaspoon freshly ground black pepper
Pinch of nutmeg
12 ounces Gruyère cheese, grated (5 cups)
½ cup freshly grated Parmesan cheese
16 slices white sandwich bread, crusts removed
Dijon mustard
8 ounces baked Virginia ham, sliced but not paper thin

I use Pepperidge Farm white bread.

Preheat the oven to 400 degrees.

Melt the butter over low heat in a small saucepan and add the flour all at once, stirring with a wooden spoon for 2 minutes. Slowly pour the hot milk into the butter–flour mixture and cook, whisking constantly, until the sauce is thickened. Off the heat add the salt, pepper, nutmeg, ½ cup grated Gruyère, and the Parmesan and set aside.

To toast the bread, place the slices on two baking sheets and bake for 5 minutes. Turn each slice and bake for another 2 minutes, until toasted.

Lightly brush half the toasted breads with mustard, add a slice of ham to each, and sprinkle with half the remaining Gruyère. Top with another piece of toasted bread. Slather the tops with the cheese sauce, sprinkle with the remaining Gruyère, and bake the sandwiches for 5 minutes. Turn on the broiler and broil for 3 to 5 minutes, or until the topping is bubbly and lightly browned. Serve hot.

Blue Cheese Soufflé

SERVES 2 TO 3

This really has the WOW! factor. I was a little afraid to attempt a souf-
flé (think Audrey Hepburn in Sabrina*) but after you've made this once,*
you'll agree that it's really easy and so delicious. I generally hate recipes
that say "serve immediately," but this is worth it.

3 tablespoons unsalted butter, plus extra for greasing
    the dish
¼ cup finely grated Parmesan cheese, plus extra for
    sprinkling
3 tablespoons all-purpose flour
1 cup scalded milk
Kosher salt and freshly ground black pepper
Pinch of cayenne pepper
Pinch of nutmeg
4 extra-large egg yolks, at room temperature
3 ounces good Roquefort cheese, chopped
5 extra-large egg whites, at room temperature
⅛ teaspoon cream of tartar

Preheat the oven to 400 degrees. Butter the inside of an 8-cup
soufflé dish (7½ inches in diameter × 3¼ inches deep) and
sprinkle evenly with Parmesan.

Melt the butter in a small saucepan over low heat. With a
wooden spoon, stir in the flour and cook, stirring constantly, for
2 minutes. Off the heat, whisk in the hot milk, ½ teaspoon
salt, ¼ teaspoon black pepper, the cayenne, and nutmeg. Cook
over low heat, whisking constantly, for 1 minute, until smooth
and thick.

Off the heat, while still hot, whisk in the egg yolks, one at a
time. Stir in the Roquefort and the ¼ cup of Parmesan and
transfer to a large mixing bowl.

Put the egg whites, cream of tartar, and a pinch of salt in the bowl of an electric mixer fitted with the whisk attachment. Beat on low speed for 1 minute, on medium speed for 1 minute, then finally on high speed until they form firm, glossy peaks.

Whisk one quarter of the egg whites into the cheese sauce to lighten and then fold in the rest. Pour into the soufflé dish, then smooth the top. Draw a large circle on top with the spatula to help the soufflé rise evenly, and place in the middle of the oven. Turn the temperature down to 375 degrees. Bake for 30 to 35 minutes (don't peek!) until puffed and brown. Serve immediately.

To make in advance, prepare the recipe through adding the cheeses up to 2 hours ahead. Keep covered at room temperature and then proceed with the recipe just before baking.

Salad with
Warm Goat Cheese

MAKES 4 SALADS

Jeffrey and I ate this for lunch at our local café and I ran home to try it myself. It's easy enough to make for a quiet lunch alone and elegant enough for company. Ask your cheese shop for small, round fresh goat cheese (chévres) crottins; they're flavorful but soft enough to melt onto the bread.

> 3 or 4 fresh small goat cheeses (*crottins*)
> 8 slices of country white bread
> Good olive oil
> Salad greens for 4 salads
> Vinaigrette (page 102)
> Kosher salt
> Freshly ground black pepper

Any assortment of flavorful greens is good for this salad.

Preheat the oven to 450 degrees.

Cut each *crottin* horizontally into 2 or 3 half-inch slices. Place the bread on a baking sheet, brush lightly with olive oil, and place a slice of goat cheese on each piece of bread. Bake for 8 to 10 minutes, until the bread is toasted and the cheese is warm.

Meanwhile, place the salad greens in a large bowl and toss with enough vinaigrette to moisten. Divide the salad among 4 lunch plates. Place 2 slices of toasted bread on each salad, sprinkle with salt and pepper, and serve.

Eggplant Gratin

SERVES 4

The first time my husband took me to Paris we splurged on a restaurant called Le Coupe-Chou. Jeffrey had a delicious eggplant gratin, which he's been asking me to make ever since. This version of that dish was inspired by Richard Olney in his wonderful book Simple French Food.

Good olive oil, for frying
1½ pounds eggplant, unpeeled, sliced ½ inch thick
½ cup ricotta cheese
2 extra-large eggs
½ cup half-and-half
1 cup freshly grated Parmesan cheese, divided
Kosher salt
Freshly ground black pepper
1 cup good bottled marinara sauce, such as Rao's

Preheat the oven to 425 degrees.

Heat about ⅛ inch of olive oil in a very large frying pan over medium heat. When the oil is almost smoking, add several slices of eggplant and cook, turning once, until they are evenly browned on both sides and cooked through, about 5 minutes. Be careful, it splatters! Transfer the cooked eggplant slices to paper towels to drain. Add more oil, heat it, and add more eggplant until all the slices are cooked.

Meanwhile, in a small bowl, mix together the ricotta, eggs, half-and-half, ½ cup of the Parmesan, ¼ teaspoon salt, and ¼ teaspoon pepper.

In each of four individual gratin dishes, place a layer of eggplant slices, then sprinkle with Parmesan, salt, and pepper and spoon on ¼ cup of the marinara sauce. Next, add a second layer of eggplant, more salt and pepper, one quarter of the ricotta mixture, and finally a tablespoon of grated Parmesan on top.

Place the gratins on a baking sheet and bake for 10 minutes; lower the heat to 375 degrees and bake for another 20 minutes, or until the custard sets and the top is browned. Serve warm.

If you don't have small gratin dishes, layer the eggplant slices and other ingredients in one large shallow dish and bake until hot and bubbly.

Pissaladière

PROVENÇAL PIZZA

EACH PIZZA SERVES 4 TO 5

Many dishes from Provence take their inspiration from Italy, which is right next door. Pissaladière is usually made in a large rectangle like a tart. It's great with a salad and a glass of wine for a light summer lunch. You can certainly skip the anchovies. This recipe makes enough dough for two pizzas, so double the topping or freeze one dough for another time.

For the topping (makes 1 pissaladière)
¼ cup good olive oil, plus extra for brushing
2 pounds yellow onions, halved and sliced ¼ inch thick
1 tablespoon fresh thyme leaves
1½ teaspoons kosher salt
½ teaspoon freshly ground black pepper
2 whole cloves of garlic

For the dough (makes 2 pissaladières)
1¼ cups warm (100 to 110 degrees) water
2 envelopes dry yeast
1 tablespoon honey
3 tablespoons good olive oil
4 cups all-purpose flour, plus extra for kneading
2 teaspoons kosher salt

To assemble each pissaladière
Cornmeal, for baking
12 to 18 anchovy fillets
12 French black olives, preferably oil-cured, pitted

For the topping, heat the olive oil in a very large sauté pan and cook the onions, thyme, salt, pepper, and garlic over low heat for 45 minutes, until the onions are sweet and cooked but not browned. Toss the onions from time to time. After 30 minutes, take out the garlic, chop it roughly, and add it back to the onions.

Really good olives rarely come pitted, but it's easy to pit them yourself. Smash each olive lightly with the flat side of a knive to split, and pick out the pit.

You can make
the dough early
and refrigerate
it for up to
4 hours. Allow
it to come to
room tempera-
ture before
proceeding.

Meanwhile, for the dough, combine the water, yeast, honey, and olive oil in the bowl of an electric mixer fitted with a dough hook. (If the bowl is cold, start with warmer water so it's at least 100 degrees when you add the yeast.) Add 3 cups of the flour, then the salt, and mix on medium-low speed. While mixing, add 1 more cup of flour, or just enough to make a soft dough. Mix the dough on medium-low speed for about 10 minutes, until smooth, sprinkling it with flour to keep it from sticking to the bowl. When the dough is ready, turn it out onto a floured board and knead it by hand a dozen times. It should be smooth and elastic. Place the dough in a well-oiled bowl and turn it to cover lightly with oil. Cover the bowl with a damp kitchen towel. Allow to rest at room temperature for 30 minutes.

Preheat the oven to 450 degrees.

Divide the dough into 2 equal parts, rolling each one into a smooth ball. If you're only making one pissaladière, place one ball on a baking sheet and cover it loosely with a damp towel. Allow the dough to rest for 10 minutes. (If you're not using the other dough, wrap it well and refrigerate or freeze it for the next time.) Roll the dough lightly with a rolling pin, then stretch it to a 10 × 15-inch rectangle and place it on a baking sheet sprinkled with cornmeal.

Spoon the onion topping onto the dough, leaving a ¾-inch border all around. Artfully arrange the anchovies and olives on top, brush the edge of the dough with olive oil, and bake for 15 minutes, or until the crust is crisp. Serve hot on a cutting board.

This is best right out of the oven. To make ahead, prepare the dough and the onions separately, then assemble and bake the pissaladière just before serving.

Goat Cheese Tart

SERVES 6

No one has taught me more about cooking than my dear friend Anna Pump, who owns the wonderful specialty food store in Sagaponack, New York, called Loaves and Fishes. She also writes cookbooks that I use all the time. This tart is inspired by a tart in her first book, The Loaves and Fishes Cookbook.

> 1½ cups all-purpose flour, plus more for dusting the board
> Kosher salt
> 13 tablespoons cold unsalted butter, divided
> 3 to 4 tablespoons ice water
> ¾ cup chopped shallots (3 to 4 shallots)
> 10½ ounces garlic-and-herb soft goat cheese, such as Montrachet
> 1 cup heavy cream
> 3 extra-large eggs
> ¼ cup chopped basil leaves
> ⅛ teaspoon freshly ground black pepper

Preheat the oven to 350 degrees.

For the crust, put the flour and ¼ teaspoon salt in the bowl of a food processor fitted with the steel blade. Cut 12 tablespoons (1½ sticks) of the butter into large dice, add to the bowl, and pulse until the butter is the size of peas. With the machine running, add the ice water all at once and process until the dough becomes crumbly. Don't overprocess. Dump the dough out on a floured board, gather it loosely into a ball, cover with plastic wrap, and refrigerate for 30 minutes.

Roll the dough on a well-floured board and fit it into a 9-inch tart pan with a removable sides, rolling the pin over the top to cut off the excess dough. Butter one side of a square of aluminum foil and fit it, butter side down, into the tart pan. Fill the foil with rice or beans. Bake for 20 minutes. Remove the beans and foil from the tart shell, prick the bottom all over with a fork, and bake for another 10 minutes.

Meanwhile, heat the remaining tablespoon of butter in a small pan and sauté the shallots over low heat for 5 minutes, or until tender. Place the goat cheese in the bowl of the food processor and process until crumbly. Add the cream, eggs, basil, ¼ teaspoon salt, and the pepper and process until blended.

Scatter the cooked shallots over the bottom of the tart shell. Pour the goat cheese mixture over the shallots to fill the shell (if the shell has shrunk, there may be leftover filling). Bake for 30 to 40 minutes, until the tart is firm when shaken and the top is lightly browned. Allow to cool for 10 minutes and serve hot or at room temperature.

Lightly push the dough into the pan rather than stretching it, or the tart shell will shrink during baking.

Save the beans or rice for the next time you make a tart.

Scrambled Eggs with Truffles

SERVES 4 TO 5

Several years ago my dear friend Patricia Wells invited us for a "truffle" weekend. We cooked every dish for every meal with truffles—even breakfast! This dish is special for a holiday brunch, and the timing is perfect because fresh black truffles are in season in France from late December through February. Scrambled eggs made over a double boiler are so creamy that this is an elegant dish even without the truffles.

1 fresh black truffle (1 ounce)
16 extra-large eggs
1 cup half-and-half
2 teaspoons kosher salt
½ teaspoon freshly ground black pepper
4 to 5 slices brioche (page 92) or white toast, crusts
    removed and cut in half diagonally

Black truffles are French and white truffles are Italian; don't even think about using the canned ones.

Clean the truffle with a soft brush; don't wash it! Beat the eggs, half-and-half, salt, and pepper together in a heat-proof glass bowl until combined but not frothy. Shave the truffle into the egg mixture with a truffle shaver or mandoline. If you have time, cover with plastic wrap and allow to sit in the refrigerator for a few hours. The eggs will become more infused with the flavor of the truffle.

When ready to serve, set the bowl over a saucepan of simmering water, making sure the bottom of the bowl doesn't touch the water. Cook over the water, stirring occasionally with a wooden spoon, until the eggs are thick and custardy. This will take about 20 to 25 minutes. Remove from the heat immediately.

These will be creamy when done. Cook until a spoon stands up in the middle.

Place two toast points on each plate and spoon the cooked eggs on top. Serve hot.

Herbed-Baked Eggs

SERVES 4

Lots of people who knew I was writing a French cookbook wanted a recipe for omelettes. I spent days making them but my heart was never really in it because I always imagined myself cooking lunch while my friends sat waiting at the table. Rori Trovato came up with the perfect solution—shirred eggs, or herb-baked eggs. They were so delicious that we were standing with our forks ready as soon as Quentin took this photograph. It's very French and you can make them with any seasonings you like.

½ teaspoon minced fresh garlic
½ teaspoon minced fresh thyme leaves
½ teaspoon minced fresh rosemary leaves
2 tablespoons minced fresh parsley
2 tablespoons freshly grated Parmesan cheese
12 extra-large eggs
¼ cup heavy cream
2 tablespoons unsalted butter
Kosher salt
Freshly ground black pepper
Toasted French bread or brioche (page 92), for serving

Preheat the broiler for 5 minutes and place the oven rack 6 inches below the heat.

Combine the garlic, thyme, rosemary, parsley, and Parmesan cheese and set aside. Carefully crack 3 eggs into each of 4 small bowls or teacups (you won't be baking them in these) without breaking the yolks. (It's very important to have all the eggs ready to go before you start cooking.)

Place four individual gratin dishes on a baking sheet. Place 1 tablespoon of cream and ½ tablespoon of butter in each dish and place under the broiler for about 3 minutes, until hot and bubbly. Quickly, but carefully, pour 3 eggs into each gratin dish and sprinkle evenly with the herb mixture, then sprinkle liberally with salt and pepper. Place back under the broiler for 5 to 6 minutes, until the whites of the eggs are almost cooked. (Rotate the baking sheet once if they aren't cooking evenly.) The eggs will continue to cook after you take them out of the oven. Allow to set for 60 seconds and serve hot with toasted bread.

You can only make as many of these as you can fit under your broiler at once. If you use smaller, deeper dishes, adjust the cooking time.

Spinach in Puff Pastry

SERVES 6

Puff pastry is the essence of sophisticated French cooking, and it makes any filling elegant. Fortunately, Pepperidge Farm makes an excellent one that you can find in the freezer at your grocery store. This is a delicious lunch but also makes a great dinner for a guest who's vegetarian.

Defrost puff pastry overnight in the refrigerator. Be sure it's still cold when you bake it.

To toast pignolis, place in a dry sauté pan over low heat for 5 to 10 minutes, until lightly browned.

4 tablespoons (½ stick) unsalted butter
2 cups chopped onions (2 onions)
1 tablespoon chopped garlic (3 cloves)
2 (10-ounce) boxes frozen chopped spinach, defrosted
⅓ cup chopped scallions, white and green parts (2 scallions)
1 cup grated Gruyère cheese
¾ cup freshly grated Parmesan cheese
4 extra-large eggs, lightly beaten
1 tablespoon dry bread crumbs, plain or seasoned
2 teaspoons kosher salt
¾ teaspoon freshly ground black pepper
½ teaspoon ground nutmeg
¼ cup toasted pignoli (pine) nuts
2 sheets (1 box) frozen puff pastry (such as Pepperidge Farm), defrosted overnight in the refrigerator
1 extra-large egg beaten with 1 tablespoon water, for egg wash

Preheat the oven to 375 degrees.

Heat the butter in a sauté pan and cook the onions over medium-low heat for 5 to 7 minutes, until tender. Add the garlic and cook for 1 more minute. Meanwhile, squeeze most of the water out of the spinach and place it in a bowl. Add the onion mixture, scallions, Gruyère, Parmesan, eggs, bread crumbs, salt, pepper, nutmeg, and pignolis. Mix well.

Unfold one sheet of puff pastry and place it on a baking sheet lined with parchment paper. Spread the spinach mixture in the middle of the pastry, leaving a 1-inch border. Brush the border with the egg wash. Roll out the second piece of puff pastry on a floured board until it's an inch larger in each direction. Place the second sheet of pastry over the spinach and seal the edges, crimping them with a fork. Brush the top with egg wash but don't let it drip down the sides or the pastry won't rise. Make three small slits in the pastry, sprinkle with salt and pepper, and bake for 30 to 40 minutes, until the pastry is lightly browned. Transfer to a cutting board and serve hot.

This can be assembled a day in advance, refrigerated, and baked before serving.

Mussels in White Wine
MOULES MARINIÈRES

SERVES 6

Almost every bistro in Paris has its own version of mussels in white wine. This traditional country French dish takes some cutting and chopping, but most of it can be done in advance. I serve it for lunch with lots of crusty bread for dipping in the spicy broth, or for dinner ladled over a pound of cooked linguine.

A mini food processor will make short work of all the chopping.

Use a buttery white wine such as Chardonnay or Châteauneuf-du-Pape.

6½ pounds cultivated mussels
⅔ cup all-purpose flour
1 teaspoon good saffron threads
5 tablespoons unsalted butter
3 tablespoons good olive oil
2 cups chopped shallots (10 to 15 shallots)
⅓ cup minced garlic (12 to 15 cloves)
1 cup chopped canned plum tomatoes, drained (8 ounces)
¾ cup chopped flat-leaf parsley
¼ cup fresh thyme leaves
2 cups good white wine
4 teaspoons kosher salt
2 teaspoons freshly ground black pepper

To clean the mussels, put them in a large bowl with 4 quarts of water and the flour and soak for 30 minutes, or until the mussels disgorge any sand. Drain the mussels, then remove the "beard" from each with your fingers. If they're dirty, scrub the mussels with a brush under running water. Discard any mussels whose shells aren't tightly shut. Soak the saffron in ¼ cup hot tap water for 15 minutes and set aside.

In a large (12-quart) nonaluminum stockpot, heat the butter and olive oil over medium heat. Add the shallots and cook for 5 minutes; then add the garlic and cook for 3 more minutes, or until the shallots are translucent. Add the saffron with the soaking water, the tomatoes, parsley, thyme, wine, salt, and pepper. Bring to a boil.

Add the mussels, stir well, then cover the pot, and cook over medium heat for 8 to 10 minutes, until all the mussels are opened (discard any that do not open). With the lid on, shake the pot once or twice to be sure the mussels don't burn on the bottom. Pour the mussels and the sauce into a large bowl and serve hot.

Seafood Platter

SERVES 6

It seems as though every other street corner in Paris has a bistro that sells seafood platters outside that people take home for hors d'oeuvres. My friend Ngaere Seeler actually served this for lunch one hot summer day with a fresh corn salad and it was delicious. You can buy everything precooked or already prepared from the seafood shop and all you need to do is arrange it. How easy is that?

Crushed ice
24 raw oysters on the half shell
24 raw littleneck clams on the half shell
3 (1½ pounds) cooked lobsters, cut in half
24 cooked jumbo shrimp, peeled and deveined, with tails on
Cooked Dungeness crabs, quartered (optional)
Lemons, halved

Fill a large platter with crushed ice. Place the seafood artfully on top of the ice. Serve with the sauces.

MUSTARD SAUCE

MAKES 1½ CUPS

1¼ cups good mayonnaise
3 tablespoons Dijon mustard
1 tablespoon whole-grain mustard
¼ teaspoon kosher salt

Combine all the ingredients and serve with the seafood.

COCKTAIL SAUCE

MAKES 1 1/2 CUPS

1/2 cup chili sauce
1/2 cup ketchup
3 tablespoons prepared horseradish
2 teaspoons freshly squeezed lemon juice
1/2 teaspoon Worcestershire sauce
1/4 teaspoon Tabasco sauce

Combine all the ingredients and serve with the seafood.

I prefer Heinz chili sauce and ketchup.

MIGNONETTE SAUCE

MAKES 1/2 CUP

2 shallots, minced
3/4 cup good champagne vinegar or white wine vinegar
1 tablespoon sugar
1 teaspoon freshly ground black pepper
1 tablespoon fresh green herbs such as parsley, dill,
   and/or chives

Place the shallots, vinegar, and sugar in a small saucepan and bring to a boil. Cook uncovered for 1 minute. Remove from the heat and allow to cool to room temperature. Add the pepper and herbs and serve with the raw oysters.

soup
and
salad

Winter Squash Soup

Provençal Vegetable Soup

Zucchini Vichyssoise

Seafood Stew

Lentil Sausage Soup

Brioche Loaves

Celery Root Rémoulade

Endive, Pear, and Roquefort Salad

Avocado and Grapefruit Salad

Fennel Salad

Warm Mushroom Salad

Green Salad Vinaigrette

About French Flowers

I really love beautiful flower arrangements, but I usually make a mess of them on the first try. I'm having a dinner party, I'm behind schedule, and that's just when the flowers are delivered. I don't know why I always think I can just put them in a vase and have it turn out beautifully, but it never does. So, there I am, flowers everywhere, buckets filled with water all over the counter, and I'm tearing the pantry apart looking for the right vessel. It happens every time. I keep asking myself, how do French floral designers pull together the most gorgeous bouquets that are both casual and elegant at the same time? I decided to figure out their secrets.

The first thing I learned is that the French are masters of repetition. Choose one kind of flower and use lots and lots of them. On a round dinner table, one round vase packed with full-blown apricot garden roses makes a statement and looks truly sophisticated. The table is round, the vase is round, each flower is round, and the curve of the arrangement is round. All of the elements work together to create a symmetry that is both simple and elegant. Best of all, it doesn't look as though you've tortured the flowers into an arrangement; rather it looks as though you gathered them in the garden and just tossed them casually in a vase. (Only you and I will know about the chaos in the kitchen!)

I learned the second step of French flower arranging from the most famous Parisian flower designer, Christian Tortu, who turned the flower world upside down with his monochromatic arrangements. What he does is really *look* at both the color and the form of a flower—say, a white tulip—and he makes an arrangement to accentuate that flower's beauty. The petals of the tulip and the stem are both curved, so he'll use a round bowl for the arrangement, allowing the curved stems to bow gracefully from the bowl. He then accentuates the "whiteness" of the flower by adding other white flowers such as white freesia, white lilac, and white rununculas to the tulips. Taking a cue from the color of the stem of the tulip, which is actually acid green (who ever looks at the stem?), he adds lime-green alchemilla to highlight that color. It may look complex, but once you understand the concept, it's surprisingly simple, and it's really just an homage to the beauty of one perfect white tulip.

The French are masters of repetition. Choose one kind of flower and use lots and lots of them.

Winter Squash Soup
SOUPE AU POTIRON

SERVES 4

Julia Child writes that many French brides are surprised to discover that their mother-in-law's recipe for soupe au potiron *is actually made* not *with* potiron—*a French pumpkin—but rather with butternut squash. This soup approximates that French flavor by combining our American pumpkin with butternut squash. Small croutons and a sprinkling of cheese also make it very French.*

You can also make this soup in a blender.

2 tablespoons unsalted butter
1 tablespoon good olive oil
2 cups chopped yellow onions (2 onions)
1 (15-ounce) can pumpkin purée (*not* pumpkin pie filling)
1½ pounds butternut squash, peeled and cut in chunks
3 cups Homemade Chicken Stock (page 84) or canned broth
2 teaspoons kosher salt
½ teaspoon freshly ground black pepper
1 cup half-and-half
Crème fraîche, grated Gruyère, or croutons (see Note), for serving (optional)

Heat the butter and oil in a heavy-bottomed stockpot, add the onions, and cook over medium-low heat for 10 minutes, or until translucent. Add the pumpkin purée, butternut squash, chicken stock, salt, and pepper. Cover and simmer over medium-low heat for about 20 minutes, until the butternut squash is very tender. Process the mixture through the medium blade of a food mill. Return to the pot, add the half-and-half, and heat slowly. If the soup needs more flavor, add another teaspoon of salt. Serve hot with garnishes, if desired.

To serve with croutons, remove the crusts from 2 slices of white bread, cut them in ½-inch cubes, and sauté them in 1 tablespoon of butter until browned. Season with salt and pepper.

Provençal Vegetable Soup
SOUPE AU PISTOU

SERVES 6 TO 8

I first made this old-fashioned soup in the 1970s when I was studying Julia Child's cookbooks and learning about French food. It can be made with almost any vegetables you have on hand; I add zucchini (with the haricots verts) in summer or butternut squash (with the carrots) in the winter. Pistou is like Italian pesto but it's got tomato added to the basil and garlic. Serve it on the side so people can add as much as they like.

2 tablespoons good olive oil
2 cups chopped onions (2 onions)
2 cups chopped leeks, white and light green parts
    (2 to 4 leeks)
3 cups ½-inch-diced unpeeled boiling potatoes (1 pound)
3 cups ½-inch-diced carrots (1 pound)
1½ tablespoons kosher salt
1 teaspoon freshly ground black pepper
3 quarts Homemade Chicken Stock (recipe follows) or
    canned broth
1 teaspoon saffron threads
½ pound haricots verts (French string beans), ends
    removed and cut in half
4 ounces spaghetti, broken in pieces
1 cup Pistou (recipe follows)
Freshly grated Parmesan cheese, for serving

Heat the olive oil in a large stockpot, add the onions, and sauté over low heat for 10 minutes, or until the onions are translucent. Add the leeks, potatoes, carrots, salt, and pepper and sauté over medium heat for another 5 minutes. Add the chicken stock and saffron, bring to a boil, then simmer uncovered for 30 minutes, or until all the vegetables are tender. Add the haricots verts and spaghetti, bring to a simmer, and cook for 15 more minutes.

To serve, whisk ¼ cup of the pistou into the hot soup, then season to taste. Depending on the saltiness of your chicken stock, you may need to add up to another tablespoon of salt. Serve with grated Parmesan cheese and more pistou.

To make in advance, cook the soup but don't add the haricots verts, pasta, or pistou. When you're ready to serve, add the haricots and spaghetti, simmer for 15 minutes, then serve with the pistou.

HOMEMADE CHICKEN STOCK

MAKES 6 QUARTS

3 (5-pound) chickens
3 large onions, unpeeled and quartered
6 carrots, unpeeled and halved
4 celery stalks with leaves, cut in thirds
4 parsnips, unpeeled and cut in half (optional)
20 sprigs of fresh flat-leaf parsley
15 sprigs of fresh thyme
20 sprigs of fresh dill
1 head of garlic, unpeeled and cut in half crosswise
2 tablespoons kosher salt
2 teaspoons whole black peppercorns

Homemade Chicken Stock can be refrigerated for a few days or frozen for up to 6 months.

Place the chickens, onions, carrots, celery, parsnips, parsley, thyme, dill, garlic, salt, and peppercorns in a 16- to 20-quart stockpot with 7 quarts of water and bring to a boil. Skim the surface as needed. Simmer uncovered for 4 hours. Strain the entire contents of the pot through a colander, discarding the chicken and vegetables, and chill. Discard the hardened fat, and then pack the broth in quart containers.

PISTOU

MAKES 1 CUP

4 large garlic cloves
¼ cup tomato paste
24 large basil leaves
½ cup freshly grated Parmesan cheese
½ cup good olive oil

Pistou can be refrigerated for a few days or frozen for up to 6 months.

Place the garlic, tomato paste, basil, and Parmesan in the bowl of a food processor and purée. With the motor running, slowly pour the olive oil down the feed tube to make a paste. Pack into a container, pour a film of olive oil on top, and close the lid.

Zucchini Vichyssoise

SERVES 5 TO 6

This is one of the first things I made in my new kitchen in Paris. Vichyssoise is a cold potato leek soup, but I like to make things with a little twist, so I've added zucchini for a fresher taste. Serve it either hot or cold; it's a great way to use up those enormous zucchinis from your garden. A little sprinkle of chopped fresh chives at the end really wakes up the flavor.

1 tablespoon unsalted butter
1 tablespoon good olive oil
5 cups chopped leeks, white and light green parts
  (4 to 8 leeks)
4 cups chopped unpeeled white boiling potatoes (8 small)
3 cups chopped zucchini (2 zucchinis)
1½ quarts Homemade Chicken Stock (page 84) or
  canned broth
1 teaspoon kosher salt
½ teaspoon freshly ground black pepper
2 tablespoons heavy cream
Fresh chives or julienned zucchini, for garnish

Heat the butter and oil in a large stockpot, add the leeks, and sauté over medium-low heat for 5 minutes. Add the potatoes, zucchini, chicken stock, salt, and pepper; bring to a boil; then lower the heat and simmer for 30 minutes. Cool for a few minutes and then process through a food mill fitted with the medium disc. Add the cream and season to taste. Serve either cold or hot, garnished with chopped chives and/or zucchini.

Be sure to wash leeks very, very well. A little sand can ruin an otherwise delicious soup.

Zucchinis never need to be peeled, just washed.

You can also make this in a blender, which will make a finer purée than a food mill.

Seafood Stew

SERVES 6

I don't have the patience to make bouillabaisse because it always takes a whole day to make. However, I love this seafood stew because it has the same flavors and, once the stock is made, only takes about an hour. Placing a slice of toasted bread in the bottom of each bowl before you ladle in the hot soup adds that extra something.

3 tablespoons good olive oil
1½ cups chopped yellow onions (2 small)
2 cups large-diced small white potatoes
2 cups chopped fennel (1 large bulb)
2 teaspoons kosher salt
1 teaspoon freshly ground black pepper
2 cups good white wine
1 (28 ounce) can plum tomatoes, chopped
1 quart Seafood Stock (recipe follows) or store-bought fish stock
1 tablespoon chopped garlic (3 cloves)
1 teaspoon saffron threads
1 pound large shrimp, shelled and deveined (use the shells for the stock)
1 pound each halibut and bass fillets, cut in large chunks
24 mussels, cleaned
3 tablespoons Pernod
1 teaspoon grated orange zest
Toasted baguette slices, buttered and rubbed with garlic

Clean mussels by placing them in a large bowl of water with a handful of flour for about 30 minutes. Pull off the "beards."

Heat the oil in a Dutch oven or stockpot, add the onions, potatoes, fennel, salt, and pepper, and sauté over medium-low heat for 15 minutes, until the onions begin to brown. Add the wine and scrape up the brown bits with a wooden spoon. Add the tomatoes with their juices, stock, garlic, and saffron to the pot, bring to a boil, then lower the heat and simmer uncovered for 15 minutes, until the potatoes are tender. Add the shrimp, fish, and mussels, bring to a boil, then lower the heat, cover, and cook for 5 minutes. Turn off the heat and allow the pot to sit covered for another 5 minutes. The fish and shrimp should be cooked and the mussels opened. Discard any mussels that don't open. Stir in the Pernod, orange zest, and salt to taste. Serve ladled over one or two slices of toasted baguette.

To make ahead, prepare the sauce and refrigerate. Before serving, bring to a boil, add the shrimp, fish, and mussels, and proceed with the recipe.

SEAFOOD STOCK

MAKES 1 QUART

You can make this in advance and freeze it.

> 2 tablespoons good olive oil
> Shells from 1 pound large shrimp
> 2 cups chopped yellow onions (2 onions)
> 2 carrots, unpeeled and chopped
> 3 stalks celery, chopped
> 2 cloves garlic, minced
> ½ cup good white wine
> ⅓ cup tomato paste
> 1 tablespoon kosher salt
> 1½ teaspoons freshly ground black pepper
> 10 sprigs fresh thyme, including stems

Warm the oil in the pan over medium heat. Add the shrimp shells, onions, carrots, and celery over medium heat for 15 minutes, until lightly browned. Add the garlic and cook 2 more minutes. Add 1½ quarts of water, the white wine, tomato paste, salt, pepper, and thyme. Bring to a boil, then reduce the heat and simmer for 1 hour. Strain through a sieve, pressing the solids. You should have approximately 1 quart of stock. If not, you can make up the difference with water or white wine.

Lentil Sausage Soup

MAKES 4 QUARTS; SERVES 8 TO 10

In Paris, I make this soup with French sausage with truffles and pista-chios, which has a much finer texture than the Italian sausage we can find here. However, when I'm home, it's also delicious made with kiel-basa and it's so much easier to find.

1 pound French green lentils such as du Puy
¼ cup olive oil, plus extra for serving
4 cups diced yellow onions (3 large)
4 cups chopped leeks, white and light green parts only
   (2 leeks)
1 tablespoon minced garlic (2 large cloves)
1 tablespoon kosher salt
1½ teaspoons freshly ground black pepper
1 tablespoon minced fresh thyme leaves
1 teaspoon ground cumin
3 cups medium-diced celery (8 stalks)
3 cups medium-diced carrots (4 to 6 carrots)
3 quarts Homemade Chicken Stock (page 84) or canned
   broth
¼ cup tomato paste
1 pound kielbasa, cut in half lengthwise and sliced
   ⅓ inch thick
2 tablespoons dry red wine or red wine vinegar
Freshly grated Parmesan cheese, for serving

In a large bowl, cover the lentils with boiling water and allow to sit for 15 minutes. Drain.

In a large stockpot over medium heat, heat the olive oil and sauté the onions, leeks, garlic, salt, pepper, thyme, and cumin for 20 minutes, or until the vegetables are translucent and tender. Add the celery and carrots and sauté for another 10 minutes. Add the chicken stock, tomato paste, and drained lentils, cover, and bring to a boil. Reduce the heat and simmer uncovered for 1 hour, or until the lentils are cooked through and tender. Check the seasonings. Add the kielbasa and red wine and simmer until the kielbasa is hot. Serve drizzled with olive oil and sprinkled with grated Parmesan.

Brioche Loaves

MAKES 2 LOAVES

So many people have written to tell me that they couldn't find the egg bread, challah, or brioche loaf called for in some of my recipes (like the croutons in Barefoot Contessa Family Style*) that I decided to see how hard it was to make at home. I was surprised to find out it was quite easy! I usually find baking bread too time-consuming but, while this one does need to sit overnight in the refrigerator, it doesn't require all that kneading. This recipe is for two loaves, so you can freeze one for later.*

½ cup warm water (110 to 120 degrees)
1 package dried yeast
3 tablespoons sugar
6 extra-large eggs, at room temperature
4¼ cups unbleached flour
2 teaspoons kosher salt
½ pound (2 sticks) unsalted butter, at room temperature
1 egg mixed with 1 tablespoon milk, for egg wash

Be sure the butter really is at room temperature. I leave it out overnight.

Sugar feeds the yeast's growth and salt inhibits it. You want to add the sugar directly to the yeast but add the salt only after you've mixed in some flour.

Combine the water, yeast, and sugar in the bowl of an electric mixer fitted with the paddle attachment. (If the bowl is cold, start with warmer water so it's at least 110 degrees when you add the yeast.) Mix with your hands and allow to stand for 5 minutes until the yeast and sugar dissolve. Add the eggs and beat on medium speed for 1 minute, until well mixed. With the mixer on low speed, add 2 cups of the flour and the salt and mix for 5 minutes. With the mixer still on low, add 2 more cups of flour and mix for 5 more minutes. Still on low speed, add the soft butter in chunks and mix for 2 minutes, scraping down the beater, until well blended. With the mixer still running, sprinkle in the remaining ¼ cup of flour. Switch the paddle attachment to a dough hook and mix on low speed for 2 minutes. Scrape the dough into a large buttered bowl and cover with plastic wrap. Refrigerate overnight.

The next day, allow the dough to sit at room temperature for 1 hour. Grease two 8½ × 4½ × 2½-inch loaf pans. Turn the dough onto a lightly floured board and cut in half. Pat each portion into a 6 × 8-inch rectangle, then roll up each rectangle into a cylindrical loaf. Place each loaf, seam side down, into a greased pan. Cover the pans with a damp towel and set aside to rise at room temperature until doubled in volume, 2 to 2½ hours.

Preheat the oven to 375 degrees. When the loaves have risen, brush the top of each with the egg wash and bake for 45 minutes, or until the top springs back and it sounds slightly hollow when tapped. Turn the loaves out onto a wire rack to cool.

Celery Root Rémoulade

SERVES 4 TO 6

When a recipe starts with "Cut a large celery root into matchstick pieces...," I just turn the page. Who can cut a hard root vegetable that fine without slicing off their fingers? I tested lots of ways to make this salad and while you can use a mandoline, it's much easier with a food processor. One of Jeffrey's favorite things to do in Paris is to have a picnic in Luxembourg Gardens; this is a delicious salad to pack for lunch outdoors.

Make this in autumn and winter when celery root is in season.

Champagne vinegar is a good white wine vinegar

2 pounds celery root
1¾ teaspoons kosher salt
3 tablespoons freshly squeezed lemon juice
1 cup good mayonnaise
1 tablespoon Dijon mustard
1 tablespoon whole-grain mustard
2 teaspoons champagne vinegar or white wine vinegar
Pinch of freshly ground black pepper

Use a serrated knife to peel the celery root of all the brown outer portions, like peeling a pineapple. Cut the celery root into thin matchsticks with a mandoline, or grate them in a food processor fitted with the coarsest grating blade. With the food processor, press a little as you feed the chunks through and you will have larger shreds. Place the celery root in a large bowl, sprinkle with 1½ teaspoons of the salt and 2 tablespoons of lemon juice, and allow to stand at room temperature for about 30 minutes.

Meanwhile, in a small bowl whisk together the mayonnaise, the two mustards, the remaining tablespoon of lemon juice, the vinegar, the remaining ¼ teaspoon of salt, and the pepper. Add enough sauce to lightly moisten the salad. (You may have some sauce left over.) Serve cold or at room temperature.

This salad can be made a few days in advance and stored in the refrigerator.

Endive, Pear, and Roquefort Salad

SERVES 6

There are as many endive salads as there are cooks in France. You can add anything you like to complement the bitterness of the endive: watercress, prosciutto, Parmesan cheese. I sometimes get my best ideas just by looking in the refrigerator.

9 to 12 heads of Belgian endive
3 tablespoons champagne vinegar or white wine vinegar
1½ teaspoons Dijon mustard
1 extra-large egg yolk, at room temperature
1½ teaspoons kosher salt
¾ teaspoon freshly ground black pepper
¾ cup good olive oil
½ pound good Roquefort cheese
3 ripe Bartlett pears, halved, cored, and sliced
1 cup toasted walnut halves

Trim off the core end of each head of endive and slice it in half lengthwise. Cut out the cores, separate the leaves, and place 1½ to 2 heads of endive on each plate.

In a medium bowl, whisk together the vinegar, mustard, egg yolk, salt, and pepper. Slowly whisk in the olive oil to make an emulsion. Toss the pears with some vinaigrette and place on the endive. Drizzle the remaining vinaigrette over the endive leaves to moisten them. Crumble the Roquefort onto the endive. Sprinkle with walnuts and serve at room temperature.

Red or yellow Bartlett pears are both delicious.

To toast the walnut halves, place them in a dry sauté pan over medium-low heat and cook for 5 minutes, tossing frequently, until warmed through.

Avocado and Grapefruit Salad

SERVES 4

I had this delicious salad at a very elegant restaurant in Paris and I loved both its simplicity and the synergy between the avocados and the grapefruit. It's a perfect first course for a summer meal, and while you don't want to cut the avocados too far in advance, you can certainly make it before guests arrive. Choose firm but ripe avocados.

1 tablespoon Dijon mustard
¼ cup freshly squeezed lemon juice
1½ teaspoons kosher salt
¾ teaspoon freshly ground black pepper
½ cup good olive oil
3 ripe Hass avocados
3 large red grapefruits

Place the mustard, lemon juice, salt, and pepper in a small bowl. Slowly whisk in the olive oil until the vinaigrette is emulsified.

Before serving, cut the avocados in half, remove the seeds, and carefully peel off the skin. Dip each avocado half in the vinaigrette to prevent it from turning brown. Use a large, sharp knife to slice the peel off the grapefruits (be sure to remove all the white pith), then cut between the membranes to release the grapefruit segments.

Arrange the grapefruit segments on 4 small plates. Cut the avocados in wedges and arrange them with the grapefruit. Spoon a little vinaigrette on top, sprinkle with salt and pepper, and serve.

Fennel Salad

SERVES 6

I'm not crazy about raw fennel, but I think it's delicious when cooked. I wanted to make a cold fennel salad but the dilemma was how to keep some of the crunch yet have the flavor of cooked fennel. So, I decided to give some slices of fennel a quick toss in a sauté pan and—with an orange vinaigrette and a sprinkling of Parmesan—it was exactly what I was looking for.

2 pounds fennel bulbs
¼ cup plus 2 tablespoons good olive oil
¼ cup freshly squeezed orange juice
¾ teaspoon kosher salt
¼ teaspoon freshly ground black pepper
½ cup freshly grated Parmesan cheese

Cut the fronds from the fennel bulbs and reserve some of the feathery leaves for later. Cut each bulb in half and remove the cores with a sharp knife. Slice each half crosswise, making half-rounds about ¼ to ⅛ inch thick.

Heat 2 tablespoons of olive oil in a large sauté pan. Add the fennel slices and sauté for 2 to 3 minutes over medium heat, until translucent and slightly cooked but still al dente. Transfer the fennel to a bowl and set aside.

Meanwhile whisk the orange juice, salt, and pepper together in a small bowl. While whisking, slowly add ¼ cup olive oil and pour over the cooked fennel. Add the Parmesan and 2 tablespoons chopped reserved fennel leaves, and season to taste. Serve at room temperature.

Warm Mushroom Salad

SERVES 4

There's nothing particularly French about this salad except that I first had it at a bistro on Boulevard Saint-Germain-des-Prés. In fact, it's actually Italian. I hate to recommend a dish with an unusual ingredient but in this case, it's really worth it. Cremini are young cultivated mushrooms, usually brown or tan; their mature form is the portobello mushroom. Cremini have incredible flavor, and they are available at many produce stores.

1 pound cremini mushrooms
2 tablespoons unsalted butter
4 tablespoons good olive oil, divided
1 teaspoon kosher salt
$\frac{1}{2}$ teaspoon freshly ground black pepper
4 bunches of fresh arugula, washed and spun dry
8 slices good Italian prosciutto
2 tablespoons sherry wine vinegar
Chunk of Parmesan cheese
8 sun-dried tomatoes in oil, drained and julienned
Fresh flat-leaf parsley leaves

Clean the mushrooms by brushing the tops with a clean sponge. Don't wash them! Remove and discard the stems and slice the caps $\frac{1}{4}$ to $\frac{1}{2}$ inch thick.

In a large sauté pan, heat the butter and 2 tablespoons of the olive oil until bubbly. Add the mushrooms, salt, and pepper to the pan, and sauté for 3 minutes over medium heat, tossing frequently. Reduce the heat to low and sauté for another 2 to 3 minutes, until cooked through.

Meanwhile, arrange the arugula on 4 lunch plates and cover each portion with 2 slices of prosciutto. When the mushrooms are cooked, add the sherry vinegar and the remaining 2 table-spoons of olive oil to the hot pan. Spoon the mushrooms and sauce on top of the prosciutto. With a vegetable peeler, make large shavings of Parmesan cheese and place on top of the hot mushrooms. Sprinkle with the sun-dried tomatoes, parsley leaves, salt, and pepper, and serve warm.

Green Salad Vinaigrette

SERVES 6 TO 8

Cleaned mesclun mix, a mix of baby lettuces, has become so readily available that it makes serving a green salad really easy. Of course, a mixed green salad of lettuces, peppery arugula, bitter endive, and red radicchio may be a little more trouble but it also has lots of flavor. Serve this with some cheese after the main course if you want to do it as the French would!

If you're worried about eating raw egg, just eliminate it.

When you're serving a salad for a dinner party, put the vinaigrette in the bottom of a serving bowl and place the greens on top. This can sit for an hour or two until you're ready to toss and serve it.

To prepare the salad greens early, wash and spin them dry in a salad spinner and store refrigerated in a plastic bag lined with a paper towel.

For the vinaigrette
3 tablespoons champagne vinegar or white wine vinegar
1/2 teaspoon Dijon mustard
1/2 teaspoon minced fresh garlic
1 extra-large egg yolk, at room temperature
3/4 teaspoon kosher salt
1/4 teaspoon freshly ground black pepper
1/2 cup good olive oil

Salad greens or mesclun mix for 6 to 8 people

In a small bowl, whisk together the vinegar, mustard, garlic, egg yolk, salt, and pepper. While whisking, slowly add the olive oil until the vinaigrette is emulsified.

Toss the greens with enough dressing to moisten and serve immediately.

dinner

Lemon Chicken with Croutons

Chicken with Forty Cloves of Garlic

Roast Duck

Chicken with Morels

Loin of Pork with Green Peppercorns

Boeuf Bourguignon

Filet of Beef au Poivre

Steak with Béarnaise Sauce

Veal Chops with Roquefort Butter

Roast Lamb with White Beans

Rack of Lamb Persillade

Roasted Striped Bass

Scallops Provençal

Salmon with Lentils

About French Cookware

One of my first memories of Paris is of visiting the famous cookware store, Dehillerin ("Day-le-ran"). Dehillerin is the top restaurant supply store for all Parisian chefs and it's located in the area called Les Halles, where the wholesale food market used to be. I went there during my camping trip with Jeffrey to buy a small French pot for cooking dinner in our little tent. Little did I know that this would be the start of a lifelong obsession! What I've discovered since that first pot is that good cookware not only enhances the quality of my cooking, but it's also an incredible joy to use.

I recently had the pleasure of spending an evening at my East Hampton house with Chuck Williams, the founder of the Williams-Sonoma stores, who related a similar story. It was the early 1950s, when he was a building contractor in Sonoma, California. He loved to cook and he decided to go on vacation to Paris, where he fell in love with French cookware. The rest, as they say, is history, and his stores are some of the best resources for French cookware.

What makes French cookware so irresistible is that it is made to last. It's not about disposable products; it's about buying things you can use for a lifetime and then pass on to your children. If you go to Dehillerin, you'll see heavy-duty pots, great quality knives, and sturdy baking pans that really work. Wooden shelves are piled high with every kind of tart pan you can imagine—square, round, oval, big, and small. There are white porcelain baking dishes and orange Le Creuset pots in every size. Visiting the store is a memorable experience, but if you can't get there you can order online at E-Dehillerin.fr.

Of course even having the world's best cookware can't ensure a perfect dinner. That night I had Chuck over for dinner I decided to make the Kitchen Clambake from my first cookbook because it's casual and makes a great party. We all sat around the table in chef's aprons and dove into big bowls of shrimp, clams, mussels, potatoes, and sausages. It was really fun. The next morning my husband woke up and said, "That was a really delicious dinner . . . but I don't remember eating a lobster." I bolted up in bed and exclaimed, "I put them in the oven to keep warm and they're still there!" I know we've all realized at the end of a dinner party that we've forgotten to serve the bread or the salad, but this was the first time I forgot to serve the main course!

Good cookware not only enhances the quality of my cooking, but it's also an incredible joy to use.

Lemon Chicken
with Croutons

SERVES 3 TO 4

I don't know how authentically French this is, but a friend made it for us in Provence and to me it's the essence of French country cooking. A simple roast chicken is sliced onto a bed of warm croutons so they soak up all those delicious juices. How good is that? In Paris I use Poilâne bread for the croutons, but you can use any flavorful French bread.

I use Bell and Evans chickens.

1 (4- to 5-pound) roasting chicken
1 large yellow onion, sliced
Good olive oil
Kosher salt
Freshly ground black pepper
2 lemons, quartered
2 tablespoons unsalted butter, melted
6 cups (¾-inch) bread cubes (1 baguette or round boule)

Preheat the oven to 425 degrees.

Take the giblets out of the chicken and wash it inside and out. Remove any excess fat and leftover pinfeathers. Toss the onion with a little olive oil in a small roasting pan. Place the chicken on top and sprinkle the inside of the cavity with salt and pepper. Place the lemons inside the chicken. Pat the outside of the chicken dry with paper towels, brush it with the melted butter, and sprinkle with salt and pepper. Tie the legs together with kitchen string and tuck the wing tips under the body of the chicken.

Roast for 1¼ to 1½ hours, or until the juices run clear when you cut between the leg and the thigh. Cover with foil and allow to sit at room temperature for 15 minutes. (The onions may burn, but the flavor is good.)

Meanwhile, heat a large sauté pan with 2 tablespoons of olive oil until very hot. Lower the heat to medium-low and sauté the bread cubes, tossing frequently, until nicely browned, 8 to 10 minutes. Add more olive oil, as needed, and sprinkle with ½ teaspoon salt and ¼ teaspoon pepper. Place the croutons on a serving platter. Slice the chicken and place it, plus all the pan juices, over the croutons. Sprinkle with salt and serve warm.

Chicken with
Forty Cloves of Garlic

SERVES 6

I know it sounds outrageous to cook chicken with forty cloves of garlic, but the garlic becomes very sweet and tender when it's cooked for a long time. This is great to serve for a party with Moroccan Couscous (page 158) because not only are they delicious together but they can both be prepared a day ahead and reheated.

3 whole heads garlic, about 40 cloves
2 (3½-pound) chickens, cut into eighths
Kosher salt
Freshly ground black pepper
1 tablespoon unsalted butter
2 tablespoons good olive oil
3 tablespoons Cognac, divided
1½ cups dry white wine
1 tablespoon fresh thyme leaves
2 tablespoons all-purpose flour
2 tablespoons heavy cream

Choose garlic that is firm and has no green sprouts.

Separate the cloves of garlic and drop them into a pot of boiling water for 60 seconds. Drain the garlic and peel. Set aside.

Dry the chicken with paper towels. Season liberally with salt and pepper on both sides. Heat the butter and oil in a large pot or Dutch oven over medium-high heat. In batches, sauté the chicken in the fat, skin side down first, until nicely browned, about 3 to 5 minutes on each side. Turn with tongs or a spatula; you don't want to pierce the skin with a fork. If the fat is burning, turn the heat down to medium. When a batch is done, transfer it to a plate and continue to sauté all the chicken in batches. Remove the last chicken to the plate and add all of the garlic to the pot. Lower the heat and sauté for 5 to 10 minutes, turning often, until evenly browned. Add 2 tablespoons of the Cognac and the wine, return to a boil, and scrape the brown bits from the bottom of the pan. Return the chicken to the pot with the juices and sprinkle with the thyme leaves. Cover and simmer over the lowest heat for about 30 minutes, until all the chicken is done.

To prepare ahead, refrigerate the chicken with the sauce and reheat over low heat before serving.

Remove the chicken to a platter and cover with aluminum foil to keep warm. In a small bowl, whisk together ½ cup of the sauce and the flour and then whisk it back into the sauce in the pot. Raise the heat, add the remaining tablespoon of Cognac and the cream, and boil for 3 minutes. Add salt and pepper to taste; it should be very flavorful because chicken tends to be bland. Pour the sauce and the garlic over the chicken and serve hot.

Roast Duck

SERVES 4 TO 6

2 ducks (5 to 6 pounds each), innards and wing tips
   removed
6 quarts canned chicken broth
Kosher salt
Freshly ground black pepper

Allow the ducks to sit at room temperature for 20 minutes. With a fork, prick the skin all over, especially the legs, without piercing the meat, which will allow the fat to drain off while the ducks cook.

Meanwhile, in a stockpot large enough to hold two ducks, heat the chicken broth with 1 tablespoon of salt until it boils. Add the ducks very carefully and bring the broth back to a boil. If there isn't enough broth to cover the ducks, add the hottest tap water to cover. Place a plate on top of the ducks to keep them submerged. When the broth comes back to a boil, lower the heat and simmer the ducks for 45 minutes.

Skim off enough duck fat from the top of the stock to pour a film on the bottom of a large roasting pan. This will keep the ducks from sticking while they roast. Carefully take the ducks out of the stock, holding them over the pot to drain. Place them in the roasting pan, pat the skin dry with paper towels, and sprinkle each with ½ teaspoon salt and ½ teaspoon pepper.

Meanwhile, preheat the oven to 500 degrees. (Be sure your oven is very clean or it will smoke!) Roast the ducks for 30 minutes. Remove from the oven and allow them to rest, covered with aluminum foil, for 20 minutes. Serve warm.

Because ducks are so fatty, whenever I think of roasting one I have visions of smoke billowing out of the oven and the fire department on the way. Barbara Kafka solved all that in her wonderful book, Roasting.

Freeze the chicken-duck stock for up to a month to use the next time you make roast duck.

Chicken with Morels

SERVES 6

In autumn, the street markets in Paris always offer so many fresh wild mushrooms for sale that I'm overwhelmed trying to choose. Morels have lots of flavor and the dried ones we can find here in a specialty food store are just as good as the fresh ones. My friend Anna Pump, who is the master of the simple, elegant recipe, has this dish in her wonderful book, The Loaves and Fishes Cookbook. *I make it in advance and reheat it before dinner.*

Dried morels are easier to find than fresh ones.

Chicken breasts from a butcher are often much larger than those from the grocery store. Adjust the cooking time accordingly.

1 ounce dried morels, soaked for 30 minutes in 3 cups
    very hot water
6 boneless, skinless chicken breasts
Kosher salt
Freshly ground black pepper
All-purpose flour, for dredging
¼ cup clarified butter (page 33)
⅓ cup chopped shallots (2 large)
1 tablespoon minced garlic (3 cloves)
1 cup Madeira wine
1 cup (8 ounces) crème fraîche
1 cup heavy cream
2 tablespoons freshly squeezed lemon juice

Preheat the oven to 375 degrees.

Lift the morels carefully from the hot water in order to leave any grit behind in the liquid. Rinse a few times to be sure all the grittiness is gone. Discard the liquid and dry the morels lightly with paper towels. Set aside.

Sprinkle the chicken breasts with salt and pepper. Dredge them in flour and shake off the excess. Heat half the clarified butter in a large sauté pan and cook the chicken in 2 batches over medium-low heat until browned on both sides, 8 to 10 minutes. Remove to an ovenproof casserole.

Add the rest of the clarified butter to the pan along with the shallots, drained morels, and garlic. Sauté over medium heat for 2 minutes, tossing and stirring constantly. Pour the Madeira into the pan and reduce the liquid by half over high heat, 2 to 4 minutes. Add the crème fraîche, cream, lemon juice, 1 teaspoon salt, and ¾ teaspoon pepper. Boil until the mixture starts to thicken, 5 to 10 minutes. Pour the sauce over the chicken and bake for 12 minutes, or until the chicken is heated through.

To make ahead, refrigerate the chicken and sauce in the casserole and reheat slowly on top of the stove.

Loin of Pork
with Green Peppercorns

SERVES 8

A whole roasted loin of pork is big and dramatic, so it's great for a party. Since green peppercorns are such an important ingredient, you want to choose the best Madagascar peppercorns, which come brined in a can.

Ask the butcher for a "Frenched" loin of pork with chine and feather bones removed.

1 pork loin, bone in, Frenched and tied (about 5 pounds, 10 bones)
2 tablespoons good olive oil
4 teaspoons Dijon mustard, divided
4 teaspoons whole-grain mustard, divided
1 teaspoon ground fennel seed (see Note)
Kosher salt
Freshly ground black pepper
3 tablespoons all-purpose flour
1 cup good white wine
3 cups Homemade Chicken Stock (page 84) or canned broth
¼ cup green peppercorns in brine, drained

I use a Krups mini coffee grinder to grind the fennel seeds. You can also use a mortar and pestle.

Preheat the oven to 400 degrees. Allow the pork to stand at room temperature for 30 minutes.

To test the internal temperature of meat, put the thermometer into the center at the end of the meat, rather than into the top of it.

Place the pork, fat side up, in a roasting pan just large enough to hold it comfortably. In a small bowl, whisk together the olive oil, 2 teaspoons of each mustard, the fennel seed, 2 teaspoons salt, and ½ teaspoon black pepper. Rub the mixture on top of the pork and roast for 1 to 1¼ hours, until the internal temperature reaches 140 degrees. Remove from the oven, transfer to a cutting board, and cover tightly with aluminum foil for 20 minutes.

For the sauce, remove all but ¼ cup of fat from the roasting pan. If there isn't ¼ cup, add enough butter to the pan to make

¼ cup total. Over medium heat, whisk the flour into the fat in the pan and cook for 1 minute. Add the wine and scrape up all the brown bits from the bottom of the pan. Add the chicken stock, the remaining 2 teaspoons of each mustard, the green peppercorns, 2 teaspoons salt, and ½ teaspoon black pepper. Bring to a boil, then lower the heat to a simmer for 5 to 10 minutes, until the sauce is reduced and slightly thickened.

Don't allow the pork to rest under the foil for more than 20 minutes or it will overcook.

Remove the strings from the roast pork, slice between the bones, and serve warm with the hot sauce.

Boeuf Bourguignon
BEEF STEW WITH RED WINE

SERVES 6

I never really liked beef bourguignon. After cooking for three hours, the meat was stringy and dry and the vegetables were overcooked. So, I tried to solve the problem and came up with a delicious stew that cooks in an hour and a half. The good news is that it's even better the second day, so it's great for entertaining.

1 tablespoon good olive oil
8 ounces good bacon, diced
2½ pounds beef chuck cut into 1-inch cubes
Kosher salt
Freshly ground black pepper
1 pound carrots, sliced diagonally into 1-inch chunks
2 yellow onions, sliced
2 teaspoons chopped garlic (2 cloves)
½ cup Cognac or good brandy
1 (750-ml) bottle good dry red wine, such as Burgundy
2 to 2½ cups canned beef broth
1 tablespoon tomato paste
1 teaspoon fresh thyme leaves
4 tablespoons (½ stick) unsalted butter,
    at room temperature, divided
3 tablespoons all-purpose flour
1 pound frozen small whole onions
1 pound mushrooms, stems discarded, caps thickly
    sliced

For serving
Country bread, toasted or grilled
1 garlic clove, cut in half
½ cup chopped fresh flat-leaf parsley (optional)

Don't wash the mushrooms, just brush them clean.

Preheat the oven to 250 degrees.

Heat the olive oil in a large Dutch oven, such as Le Creuset. Add the bacon and cook over medium heat for 8 to 10 minutes, stirring occasionally, until the bacon is lightly browned. Remove the bacon with a slotted spoon to a large plate.

Dry the beef cubes with paper towels and then sprinkle them with salt and pepper. In batches in single layers, sear the beef in the hot oil for 3 to 5 minutes, turning to brown on all sides. Remove the seared cubes to the plate with the bacon and continue searing until all the beef is browned. Set aside.

Toss the carrots, onions, 1 tablespoon of salt, and 2 teaspoons of pepper into the fat in the pan and cook over medium heat for 10 to 12 minutes, stirring occasionally, until the onions are lightly browned. Add the garlic and cook for 1 more minute. Add the Cognac, *stand back,* and ignite with a match to burn off the alcohol. Put the meat and bacon back into the pot with any juices that have accumulated on the plate. Add the wine plus enough beef broth to almost cover the meat. Add the tomato paste and thyme. Bring to a boil, cover the pot with a tight-fitting lid, and place it in the oven for about 1¼ hours, or until the meat and vegetables are very tender when pierced with a fork. Remove from the oven and place on top of the stove.

If the sauce is too thin, you can add more of the butter and flour mixture.

To make in advance, cook the stew and refrigerate. To serve, reheat to a simmer over low heat and serve with the bread and parsley.

Combine 2 tablespoons of the butter and the flour with a fork and stir into the stew. Add the frozen onions. In a medium pan, sauté the mushrooms in the remaining 2 tablespoons of butter over medium heat for 10 minutes, or until lightly browned, and then add to the stew. Bring the stew to a boil, then lower the heat and simmer uncovered for 15 minutes. Season to taste.

Rub each slice of bread on one side with garlic. For each serving, spoon the stew over a slice of bread and sprinkle with parsley.

Filet of Beef au Poivre

SERVES 6

This classic French bistro dish is a bit expensive, but it's quick to make. Most recipes call for beef demi-glace (you don't even want to know how long it takes to make that!) but I think this has all the flavor without the hassle. Serve it with Matchstick Potatoes (page 153) and your friends will think they're in Paris.

6 filets mignon, cut 1¼ inches thick
Kosher salt
2 tablespoons coarsely ground black pepper
3½ tablespoons unsalted butter, divided
1½ tablespoons olive oil
¾ cup chopped shallots (3 to 4 shallots)
1 cup canned beef broth
½ cup good Cognac or brandy

For coarsely ground black pepper, I grind whole peppercorns in a small coffee grinder.

Place the filets on a board and pat them dry with paper towels. Sprinkle the filets with salt and then press the black pepper evenly on both sides. Allow to rest at room temperature for 15 minutes.

Heat 1½ tablespoons of the butter and the oil in a large sauté pan over medium-high heat until the butter almost smokes. Place the steaks in the pan and lower the heat to medium. Sauté the steaks for 4 minutes on one side and then for 3 minutes on the other side, for medium rare. Remove the steaks to a serving platter and cover tightly with aluminum foil.

Meanwhile, pour all but 1 tablespoon of fat from the sauté pan. Add the shallots and cook over medium heat for 2 minutes. Add the beef broth and cook over high heat for 4 to 6 minutes, until reduced by half, scraping the brown bits from the bottom of the pan. Add the Cognac and cook for 2 more minutes. Off the heat, swirl in the remaining 2 tablespoons of butter and ½ teaspoon salt. Serve the steaks hot with the sauce poured on top.

If the butcher has tied string around the filets to keep their shape, remove it before serving.

Steak with Béarnaise Sauce

SERVES 6

Béarnaise sauce, like hollandaise, usually needs to be made at the last minute, which is a problem when entertaining. I experimented and found a way to make this sauce ahead and it's every bit as delicious. Buy a good aged steak from a butcher; it makes all the difference.

For the sauce
¼ cup champagne vinegar
¼ cup good white wine
2 tablespoons minced shallots
3 tablespoons chopped fresh tarragon leaves
Kosher salt
Freshly ground black pepper
3 extra-large egg yolks
½ pound (2 sticks) unsalted butter, melted

6 (1-inch-thick) rib-eye steaks
Kosher salt
Coarsely ground black pepper
Olive oil

For the sauce, put the champagne vinegar, white wine, shallots, 1 tablespoon of the tarragon leaves, ¼ teaspoon salt, and ¼ teaspoon pepper in a small saucepan. Bring to a boil and simmer over medium heat for about 5 minutes, until the mixture is reduced to a few tablespoons. Cool slightly.

Place the cooled mixture with the egg yolks and 1 teaspoon salt in the jar of a blender and blend for 30 seconds. With the blender on, slowly pour the hot butter through the opening in the lid. Add the remaining 2 tablespoons of tarragon leaves and blend only for a second. If the sauce is too thick, add a tablespoon of white wine to thin. Keep at room temperature while you cook the steaks.

Season the steaks liberally with salt and coarsely ground black pepper on both sides. Heat a thin layer of olive oil in a large sauté pan over high heat until it's almost smoking, then sear the steaks on each side for 1 minute. Reduce the heat to low and cook the steaks for about 7 to 10 minutes, turning once, until very rare in the middle. Remove to a plate, cover tightly with aluminum foil, and allow to sit for 10 minutes. Serve with the béarnaise sauce on the side.

You can make the sauce up to an hour in advance and allow it to sit in the blender. Before serving, add 1 tablespoon of the hottest tap water and blend for a few seconds.

Veal Chops with Roquefort Butter

SERVES 8

The challenge of French cooking is how to make a sauce without the last-minute cooking. Flavored butters are a great option; they can be made days in advance or kept in the freezer for months. One or two slices on a grilled veal chop makes a delicious sauce as the butter melts onto the warm chop.

"Société B" is a very good brand of Roquefort that is available in most cheese stores.

4 tablespoons (½ stick) unsalted butter, at room temperature
2 ounces good Roquefort cheese
1 tablespoon chopped scallions
8 (1-inch-thick) veal chops
Kosher salt
Freshly ground black pepper

Place the butter and Roquefort cheese in the bowl of an electric mixer fitted with the paddle attachment and mix on medium speed until smooth. Add the scallions and mix until combined. Cut a strip of parchment paper 4½ inches wide and place the mixture on the short end of the paper. Roll into a log about 1 inch in diameter, rolling the parchment paper around the butter mixture. Chill.

Sprinkle both sides of the veal chops generously with salt and pepper. Allow to sit at room temperature for 15 to 30 minutes. Meanwhile, prepare a charcoal grill with hot coals. When the coals are hot, grill the chops for 6 to 8 minutes on each side, until almost cooked through. Remove to a platter and cover with aluminum foil. Allow to rest for 15 minutes. Serve with 1 or 2 slices of cold Roquefort butter on each chop.

Roast Lamb with White Beans

SERVES 6 TO 8

Lamb and white beans are a classic French combination. If I don't want to spend all day making lamb stew or cassoulet, I roast a boneless leg of lamb and serve it with flavorful herbed white beans. If you have a butcher bone the lamb for you, ask him to leave the end of the shank. It will help the lamb keep its shape. The beans can be made in advance and reheated.

14 ounces dried Great Northern beans, soaked overnight
   in the refrigerator
1 quart Homemade Chicken Stock (page 84)
   or canned broth
Kosher salt
4½ pound boneless leg of lamb
2½ tablespoons minced garlic (4 cloves)
3½ tablespoons minced fresh rosemary leaves
2 tablespoons plus 2 teaspoons minced fresh thyme leaves
1 tablespoon Dijon mustard, plus more for brushing
Freshly ground black pepper
3 carrots, peeled and cut into 2-inch chunks
¼ cup good olive oil
2 cups chopped yellow onions (2 onions)
1 cup medium-diced carrots (2 carrots)
1 cup medium-diced celery (2 stalks)
¼ cup fresh chopped parsley, plus more for sprinkling
⅓ cup freshly grated Parmesan cheese, plus more for
   sprinkling

Preheat the oven to 400 degrees.

Drain the beans, place in a large saucepan with the chicken stock, and bring to a boil. Lower the heat and simmer the beans in the stock for 30 to 40 minutes, until tender but not mushy. Add 1 tablespoon of salt for the last 10 minutes of cooking.

While the beans cook: If the lamb comes in a mesh covering, remove it and open the lamb flat on a work surface with the inside facing up. Trim off any large chunks of fat or membranes while keeping the meat as intact as possible.

Combine 1½ tablespoons of the garlic, 1½ tablespoons of the rosemary, 2 teaspoons of the thyme, the mustard, 2 teaspoons of salt, and ½ teaspoon of pepper in a small bowl. Smear the mixture evenly over the exposed surface of the lamb. Fold the two side flaps of meat back toward the center and tie the roast with kitchen string. (Don't overlap the flaps or it will cook unevenly).

Place the lamb seam side down on a roasting pan. Brush the outside lightly with mustard, then sprinkle evenly with ¾ teaspoon of salt and ¼ teaspoon of pepper. Add the carrot chunks to the pan and roast for about 1 hour and 15 minutes, or until an instant-read thermometer registers 130 degrees at the thickest part of the roast for rare (the ends will be better done for those who prefer medium). Remove the lamb from the oven, cover the pan tightly with aluminum foil, and allow to rest for 10 to 15 minutes.

Meanwhile, in a 12-inch sauté pan, heat the olive oil, then add the onions, diced carrots, and celery, and cook over low heat for 10 to 15 minutes, until tender. Add the parsley, the remaining 1 tablespoon of garlic, 2 tablespoons of rosemary, and 2 tablespoons of thyme and cook for 1 more minute. Add the beans and 2 cups of the cooking stock. Cook for 15 minutes until the stock makes a little sauce, adding more stock if necessary. Finish with the Parmesan cheese plus salt and pepper to taste.

Remove the string and slice the lamb. Serve it with the white beans, roasted carrots, and a sprinkle of Parmesan and parsley.

Rack of Lamb Persillade

SERVES 4 TO 5

I can't tell you how many times I've made this for dinner parties in Paris. Persillade refers to a combination of minced fresh parsley and garlic that's added to a dish near the end of the cooking. Rack of lamb is easy for entertaining, and the persillade gives it lots of flavor.

2 racks of lamb, Frenched
Good olive oil
1½ teaspoons kosher salt
½ teaspoon freshly ground black pepper
2 cups loosely packed fresh flat-leaf parsley leaves
1 tablespoon chopped garlic (3 cloves)
4 tablespoons (½ stick) unsalted butter, melted
1 cup fresh white bread crumbs
2 teaspoons grated lemon zest (2 lemons)

"Frenched" means that the butcher will scrape the tough meat off the ends of the bones to give the rack of lamb a more elegant look.

Preheat the oven to 450 degrees.

Place both racks of lamb in a roasting pan, fat side up. Rub the tops with olive oil and sprinkle with the salt and pepper. Roast the lamb for 10 minutes.

Meanwhile, place the parsley, garlic, and butter in the bowl of a food processor fitted with the steel blade and process until finely minced. Add the bread crumbs and lemon zest and process for a second until combined.

Take the lamb out of the oven and quickly press the parsley mixture on top of the meat. Return immediately to the oven and roast for another 15 minutes.

Take the lamb out of the oven and cover with aluminum foil. Allow it to rest for 15 minutes, cut in double chops, and serve.

Roasted Striped Bass

SERVES 6

Many countries around the Mediterranean share culinary traditions. The tomatoes and pancetta in this dish are Italian, the olives and Pernod are French, and the saffron is Turkish. This is delicious served hot in winter or at room temperature in summer.

2 tablespoons good olive oil
1 cup chopped yellow onions
2 ounces pancetta or bacon, diced
1 tablespoon chopped garlic
1 (28-ounce) can plum tomatoes, drained and diced
1 teaspoon saffron threads
1 teaspoon kosher salt
½ teaspoon freshly ground black pepper
½ cup dry white wine
¼ cup Pernod (optional)
1 (2- to 3-pound) striped bass fillet, skin removed
1 pound large shrimp, shelled and deveined
24 mussels, cleaned and debearded
2 tablespoons chopped fresh flat-leaf parsley

Pernod is an anise-flavored liqueur that is available in most liquor stores.

Preheat the oven to 350 degrees.

Heat the oil in a medium sauté pan and sauté the onion and pancetta over medium-low heat for 10 minutes, or until the onion is translucent. Add the garlic and cook for 1 more minute. Add the tomatoes, saffron, salt, pepper, white wine, and Pernod, if using, and simmer over medium heat for 5 minutes.

Meanwhile, lay the fish in a 10 × 14-inch baking dish and sprinkle with salt and pepper. Add the shrimp and mussels to the dish. Pour the sauce over the seafood and bake uncovered for 20 to 30 minutes, until the fish and shrimp are cooked through and the mussels are open. Sprinkle with parsley and serve.

Scallops Provençal

It doesn't get any easier than this. It's about ten minutes of prep work plus five minutes in the pan and you've got dinner that will knock their socks off. I'm usually not crazy about scallops, because they tend to be bland, but this dish has lots of flavor. A little basmati rice and a glass of dry white wine ... who needs to go to Provence?

1 pound fresh bay or sea scallops
Kosher salt
Freshly ground black pepper
All-purpose flour, for dredging
4 tablespoons (½ stick) unsalted butter, divided
½ cup chopped shallots (2 large)
1 garlic clove, minced
¼ cup chopped fresh flat-leaf parsley
⅓ cup dry white wine
1 lemon, cut in half

If you're using bay scallops, keep them whole. If you're using sea scallops, cut each one in half horizontally. Sprinkle with salt and pepper, toss with flour, and shake off the excess.

In a very large sauté pan, heat 2 tablespoons of the butter over high heat until sizzling and add the scallops in one layer. Lower the heat to medium and allow the scallops to brown lightly on one side without moving them, then turn and brown lightly on the other side. This should take 3 to 4 minutes, total. Melt the rest of the butter in the pan with the scallops, then add the shallots, garlic, and parsley and sauté for 2 more minutes, tossing the seasonings with the scallops. Add the wine, cook for 1 minute, and taste for seasoning. Serve hot with a squeeze of lemon juice.

If doubling this recipe, make it in two separate pans.

Salmon with Lentils

SERVES 4

It's the crisp crust that makes this salmon taste so delicious and look so beautiful on the plate. Make sure your sauté pan is very hot before you add the fish to create that perfect sear.

½ pound French green lentils such as du Puy
¼ cup good olive oil, plus extra for salmon
2 cups chopped yellow onions
2 cups chopped leeks, white and light green parts only
1 teaspoon fresh thyme leaves
2 teaspoons kosher salt
¾ teaspoon freshly ground black pepper
1 tablespoon minced fresh garlic
1½ cups chopped celery (4 stalks)
1½ cups chopped carrots (3 carrots)
1½ cups Homemade Chicken Stock (page 84) or good canned broth
2 tablespoons tomato paste
2 tablespoons good red wine vinegar
4 (8-ounce) center-cut salmon fillets, skin removed

Place the lentils in a heat-proof bowl and cover with boiling water. Set aside for 15 minutes, then drain.

Meanwhile, heat the oil in a sauté pan, add the onions, leeks, thyme, salt, and pepper and cook over medium heat for 10 minutes, until the onions are translucent. Add the garlic and cook for 2 more minutes. Add the drained lentils, celery, carrots, chicken stock, and tomato paste. Cover and simmer over low heat for 20 minutes, until the lentils are tender. Add the vinegar and season to taste.

Preheat the oven to 450 degrees.

For the salmon, heat a dry oven-proof sauté pan over high heat for 4 minutes. Meanwhile, rub both sides of the salmon fillets with olive oil and season the tops very liberally with salt and pepper. When the pan is very hot, place the salmon fillets seasoning-sides down in the pan and cook over medium heat without moving them for 2 minutes, until very browned. Turn the fillets and place the pan in the oven for 5 to 7 minutes, until the salmon is cooked rare. Spoon a mound of lentils on each plate and place a salmon fillet on top. Serve hot.

vegetables

Asparagus with Hollandaise

Vegetable Tian

Zucchini Gratin

Tomato Rice Pilaf

Roasted Beets

Matchstick Potatoes

Brussels Sprouts Lardons

Cauliflower Gratin

Moroccan Couscous

French String Beans

Sautéed Wild Mushrooms

Potato Celery Root Purée

Caramelized Shallots

Garlic Mashed Potatoes

Herbed New Potatoes

About French Cooking Classes

One of the things I like most about Paris is the extraordinary people Jeffrey and I have gotten to know there. Two of the people we look forward to seeing most are Patricia and Walter Wells. As a writer for *The New York Times,* like Patricia, Walter was asked to move to Paris for two years. They decided it would be a great adventure, and when it was time to come back to New York, they chose to stay in Paris for just one more year. That was twenty years ago and they're still there. Now Walter is the executive editor of the *International Herald Tribune* and Patricia has written nine books about French food, including her wonderful *Food Lover's Guide to Paris,* plus restaurant reviews for the *Tribune.* She also has an amazing school for people who want to learn more about French cooking.

A few years ago, Patricia was visiting me in East Hampton and I took her to Barefoot Contessa, the store that I'd run for twenty years. I introduced her to a customer and explained to him that she runs a wonderful cooking school in France and he said, "Oh, give me your number, my wife would love to go to your school." When he walked away, Patricia said to me, "I'm sorry, I didn't quite catch his name." I said, "That was Steven Spielberg, and his wife is the actress Kate Capshaw!"

Everybody asks me about cooking schools in France, and I always tell them to go to Patricia's. It's not just that her school is extraordinary, it's also that the joy she feels about cooking is so contagious. Patricia teaches week-long classes for six to eight students, both at her farmhouse in Provence and at her atelier, or studio, in Paris. Each week is different—some focus on wine or even on cooking with truffles! But they're all a glimpse into Patricia's amazing world. Every day she takes students to her favorite places in town. Students get to see the inner workings of Poilâne, the most famous bread bakery in France; have wine tastings at La Dernière Goutte, a fabulous wine store; have cheese tastings at Barthélémy, my favorite cheese shop; and shop at the open air markets. Each day there's an excursion and a cooking class with the ingredients that everyone has gathered.

If you want to find out more about Patricia's cooking school, visit her website, PatriciaWells.com. You'll not only have a lot of fun but I guarantee you one of the most amazing weeks of your life.

Every day Patricia Wells takes students to her favorite places, such as Poilâne, plus shopping in the open-air markets.

Asparagus with Hollandaise

SERVES 6 TO 8

Hollandaise is one of those sauces that has to be made at the last minute. When I'm dressed for a party I certainly don't need to be standing over a steaming double boiler, whisking madly, while my friends are waiting patiently for dinner. This is a quick way to make hollandaise in advance and it really doesn't separate.

12 tablespoons (1½ sticks) unsalted butter
4 extra-large egg yolks, at room temperature
3 tablespoons freshly squeezed lemon juice
Kosher salt
¼ teaspoon freshly ground black pepper
2 pinches of cayenne pepper
3 pounds fresh asparagus

Thick asparagus have more flavor than thin ones. They just need to be peeled.

Melt the butter in a small saucepan. Place the egg yolks, lemon juice, 1½ teaspoons salt, the pepper, and cayenne in the jar of a blender. Blend for 15 seconds. With the blender on, slowly pour the hot butter into the blender and blend for 30 seconds, until the sauce is thick. (You can leave it in the blender at room temperature for up to 1 hour. If it is made in advance, add 1 tablespoon of hot tap water and blend for a few seconds before serving.)

To reheat the sauce after refrigerating, place the container in the microwave for a few seconds, until it's just warm enough to pour.

Remove the tough bottoms of the asparagus stalks. If they are thick, peel the stems halfway up the stalk. Blanch the asparagus in a large pot of boiling salted water for 5 to 10 minutes, depending on their thickness, until cooked through but still al dente. Remove to a platter with tongs or a wire skimmer and sprinkle with salt.

Pour the hollandaise sauce over the warm asparagus and serve.

Vegetable Tian

SERVES 4 TO 6

For this dish to look its best, you want to choose potatoes, zucchini, and tomatoes that are about the same diameter so the slices look similar. My friend Devon Fredericks made this for us in Provence and it was also delicious the next day.

Good olive oil
2 large yellow onions, cut in half and sliced
2 garlic cloves, minced
1 pound medium round potatoes, unpeeled
¾ pound zucchini
1¼ pounds medium tomatoes
1 teaspoon kosher salt
½ teaspoon freshly ground black pepper
1 tablespoon fresh thyme leaves, plus extra sprigs
2 ounces Gruyère cheese, grated

Preheat the oven to 375 degrees.

Brush a 9 × 13 × 2-inch baking dish with olive oil. In a medium sauté pan, heat 2 tablespoons of olive oil and cook the onions over medium-low heat for 8 to 10 minutes, until translucent. Add the garlic and cook for another minute. Spread the onion mixture on the bottom of the baking dish.

Slice the potatoes, zucchini, and tomatoes in ¼-inch-thick slices. Layer them alternately in the dish on top of the onions, fitting them tightly, making only one layer. Sprinkle with salt, pepper, thyme leaves, and thyme sprigs and drizzle with 1 more tablespoon of olive oil. Cover the dish with aluminum foil and bake for 35 to 40 minutes, until the potatoes are tender. Uncover the dish, remove the thyme sprigs, sprinkle the cheese on top, and bake for another 30 minutes, or until browned. Serve warm.

146   *Barefoot in Paris*

This dish multiplies very easily; use any size pan and bake for the same amount of time.

Yukon gold potatoes are particularly good.

Zucchini Gratin

SERVES 6

French cuisine is famous for all kinds of gratins—creamy potato gratins, baked sliced vegetable gratins—and most of them have a topping made with crumbs and cheese. Here's a great example. You can assemble this a day in advance and bake it just before dinner. It's good to serve with a roast but substantial enough as a main dish for a vegetarian guest.

6 tablespoons (¾ stick) unsalted butter, plus extra for topping
1 pound yellow onions, cut in half and sliced (3 large)
2 pounds zucchini, sliced ¼ inch thick (4 zucchini)
2 teaspoons kosher salt
1 teaspoon freshly ground black pepper
¼ teaspoon ground nutmeg
2 tablespoons all-purpose flour
1 cup hot milk
¾ cup fresh bread crumbs
¾ cup grated Gruyère cheese

For fresh bread crumbs, cut the crusts from white bread and process in a food processor fitted with the steel blade. Each slice will make about ¼ cup of crumbs.

Preheat the oven to 400 degrees.

Melt the butter in a very large (12-inch) sauté pan and cook the onions over low heat for 20 minutes, or until tender but not browned. Add the zucchini and cook, covered, for 10 minutes, or until tender. Add the salt, pepper, and nutmeg and cook uncovered for 5 more minutes. Stir in the flour. Add the hot milk and cook over low heat for a few minutes, until it makes a sauce. Pour the mixture into an 8 × 10-inch baking dish.

Combine the bread crumbs and Gruyère and sprinkle on top of the zucchini mixture. Dot with 1 tablespoon of butter cut into small bits and bake for 20 minutes, or until bubbly and browned.

Tomato Rice Pilaf

SERVES 6 TO 8

Okay, this is probably as close to Italian cuisine in flavoring as it is to French, but it makes a colorful addition to a plate with a hearty French stew—and soaks up all that rich sauce.

4 tablespoons good olive oil, divided
1½ cups chopped yellow onions (2 onions)
2 cups white basmati rice
Kosher or sea salt
4 cups Homemade Chicken Stock (page 84), or canned broth, heated
½ teaspoon saffron threads
1 tablespoon chopped garlic (3 cloves)
1 (28-ounce) can whole plum tomatoes, drained and large-diced
1 teaspoon freshly ground black pepper
2 tablespoons chopped fresh flat-leaf parsley
2 tablespoons freshly grated Parmesan cheese

Heat 2 tablespoons of the olive oil in a small Dutch oven or large saucepan, add the onions, and cook over low heat for 10 minutes, or until translucent but not brown. Stir in the rice and 2 teaspoons of salt and cook over low heat for 3 minutes. Add the hot stock and the saffron and cook, covered, over the lowest heat for 20 minutes, or until the rice is tender.

Meanwhile, in a medium sauté pan, heat the remaining 2 tablespoons of olive oil, add the garlic, and cook over low heat for 30 seconds. Add the drained diced tomatoes and cook for 5 minutes, stirring from time to time. When the rice is done, add the tomato mixture, ¾ teaspoon salt, the pepper, parsley, and Parmesan. Stir with a fork, season to taste, and serve hot.

San Marzano tomatoes are the best type of canned plum tomatoes. If you can't find them, regular canned whole tomatoes are better than diced tomatoes.

Roasted Beets

SERVES 6

Beets are a surprisingly popular vegetable in France. In fact, every grocery store, produce purveyor, and street market carries packages of peeled, cooked beets for French cooks to use as is. Most recipes I've seen require you to cook the beets before removing the tough outer skins, but it's so messy peeling all those hot—red—beets. I discovered that if you peel them like carrots before roasting it's so much easier!

12 beets
3 tablespoons good olive oil
1½ teaspoons fresh thyme leaves, minced
2 teaspoons kosher salt
1 teaspoon freshly ground black pepper
2 tablespoons raspberry vinegar
Juice of 1 large orange

Preheat the oven to 400 degrees.

Remove the tops and the roots of the beets and peel each one with a vegetable peeler. Cut the beets in 1½-inch chunks. (Small beets can be halved, medium ones cut in quarters, and large beets cut in eighths.)

Place the cut beets on a baking sheet and toss with the olive oil, thyme leaves, salt, and pepper. Roast for 35 to 40 minutes, turning once or twice with a spatula, until the beets are tender. Remove from the oven and immediately toss with the vinegar and orange juice. Sprinkle with salt and pepper and serve warm.

Matchstick Potatoes

Nothing says French bistro food like matchstick potatoes, and they're easy to make because you only have to fry them once. While the meat is resting, throw these into the hot oil and everything will be ready at the same time. Remember: lots of good salt!

> Peanut or canola oil
> 2 large oval Idaho potatoes, peeled
> Sea salt or kosher salt
> Minced fresh flat-leaf parsley (optional)

Preheat the oven to 350 degrees. Pour at least 1 inch of oil into a deep pot and heat it to 350 degrees.

Slice the potatoes into thin matchsticks (⅛ inch thick) with a vegetable slicer or mandoline, dropping them into a bowl of cold water as you cut. Drain the potatoes and dry them thoroughly with paper towels. Drop the potatoes in batches into the hot oil and cook for 3 to 5 minutes, until golden brown. Remove from the pot with a wire basket skimmer or slotted spoon and drain on paper towels. Place on a baking sheet, sprinkle with salt, and keep warm in the oven while you cook the rest of the potatoes.

Sprinkle the potatoes with parsley, if desired, and serve hot.

Brussels Sprouts Lardons

SERVES 6

In the autumn when Brussels sprouts are available in the market on Boulevard Raspail, Jeffrey always wants me to cook them. I'm not such a fan of boiled Brussels sprouts so I'm usually looking for a more flavorful way to prepare them. In France they might use unsmoked bacon for the lardons, but Italian pancetta is more widely available at home.

2 tablespoons good olive oil
6 ounces Italian pancetta or bacon, ¼-inch diced
1½ pounds Brussels sprouts (2 containers), trimmed and
   cut in half
¾ teaspoon kosher salt
¾ teaspoon freshly ground black pepper
¾ cup golden raisins
1¾ cups Homemade Chicken Stock (page 84) or
   canned broth

Ask the butcher to slice the pancetta ¼ inch thick.

Heat the olive oil in a large (12-inch) sauté pan and add the pancetta. Cook over medium heat, stirring often, until the fat is rendered and the pancetta is golden brown and crisp, 5 to 10 minutes. Remove the pancetta to a plate lined with a paper towel.

To make ahead, store in the refrigerator and reheat in a skillet on top of the stove.

Add the Brussels sprouts, salt, and pepper to the fat in the pan and sauté over medium heat for about 5 minutes, until lightly browned. Add the raisins and chicken stock. Lower the heat and cook uncovered, stirring occasionally, until the sprouts are tender when pierced with a knife, about 15 minutes. If the skillet becomes too dry, add a little chicken stock or water. Return the pancetta to the pan, heat through, season to taste, and serve.

Cauliflower Gratin

SERVES 4 TO 6

Vegetable gratins are wonderful for entertaining because they can be assembled in advance and then baked just before dinner. Combining cauliflower with Gruyère and Parmesan cheeses elevates a simple vegetable to "company" status.

1 (3-pound) head of cauliflower, cut into large florets
Kosher salt
4 tablespoons (½ stick) unsalted butter, divided
3 tablespoons all-purpose flour
2 cups hot milk
½ teaspoon freshly ground black pepper
¼ teaspoon grated nutmeg
¾ cup grated Gruyère cheese, divided
½ cup grated Parmesan cheese
¼ cup fresh bread crumbs

Preheat the oven to 375 degrees. Cook the cauliflower florets in a large pot of boiling salted water for 5 to 6 minutes, until tender but still firm. Drain.

Meanwhile, melt 2 tablespoons of the butter in a medium saucepan over low heat. Add the flour, stirring constantly with a wooden spoon for 2 minutes. Pour the hot milk into the butter-flour mixture and stir until it comes to a boil. Boil, whisking constantly, for 1 minute, or until thickened. Off the heat, add 1 teaspoon of salt, the pepper, nutmeg, ½ cup of the Gruyère, and the Parmesan cheese.

This will also fit in a 9-inch round gratin dish.

Pour one third of the sauce on the bottom of an 8 × 11 × 2-inch baking dish. Place the drained cauliflower on top and then spread the rest of the sauce evenly on top. Combine the bread crumbs with the remaining ¼ cup of Gruyère and sprinkle on top. Melt the remaining 2 tablespoons of butter and drizzle over the gratin. Sprinkle with salt and pepper. Bake for 25 to 30 minutes, until the top is browned. Serve hot or at room temperature.

Moroccan Couscous

SERVES 6 TO 8

Morocco used to be part of the French empire—just think about them singing "La Marseillaise" in the movie Casablanca—*so Moroccan cuisine is everywhere in Paris. All you need is lemon roast chicken (page 110) or lamb persillade (page 132) with this couscous and you've got a quick dinner for company.*

2 cups (¾-inch) diced butternut squash
2 cups chopped yellow onion (2 onions)
1½ cups (¾-inch) diced carrots (4 carrots)
1½ cups (¾-inch) diced zucchini (2 medium)
2 tablespoons good olive oil
Kosher salt
Freshly ground black pepper
1½ cups Homemade Chicken Stock (page 84) or
   canned broth
2 tablespoons unsalted butter
¼ teaspoon ground cumin
½ teaspoon saffron threads
1½ cups couscous (10 ounces)
2 scallions, white and green parts, chopped

Preheat the oven to 375 degrees.

Place the butternut squash, onions, carrots, and zucchini on a baking sheet and toss with the olive oil, 2 teaspoons salt, and 1 teaspoon pepper. Roast for 25 to 30 minutes, until all the vegetables are tender, turning once with a spatula.

Meanwhile, in a small saucepan, bring the chicken stock to a boil and turn off the heat. Add the butter, 1 teaspoon salt (depending on saltiness of the stock), ½ teaspoon pepper, the cumin, and saffron threads and allow to steep for at least 15 minutes.

Bring the chicken stock just back to a boil. Place the couscous and cooked vegetables in a large bowl and pour the hot chicken stock over them. Cover tightly with plastic wrap and allow to stand at room temperature for 15 minutes. Add the scallions, toss the couscous and vegetables with a fork, and serve warm or at room temperature.

French String Beans
HARICOTS VERTS

SERVES 6

When I was a kid there used to be an implement at the other end of a carrot peeler that allowed the housewife of the 1950s to "French" string beans. American string beans are thicker and tougher than French ones, but we thought we could make French string beans by slicing ours lengthwise. Forget about it. French string beans are long, thin, and tender. You should be able to find them in a fancy grocery or produce store.

> 1 pound French string beans, both ends removed
> Kosher salt
> 1 red onion, large-diced
> ½ red pepper, large-diced
> ½ yellow pepper, large-diced
> Good olive oil
> Freshly ground black pepper

Preheat the oven to 425 degrees.

Blanch the string beans in a large pot of boiling salted water for just 4 minutes. Drain immediately and immerse in a large bowl of ice water to stop the cooking. When they are cool, drain and set aside.

Meanwhile, in a large bowl toss the onion and bell peppers together with 2 tablespoons of olive oil and sprinkle generously with salt and pepper. Place in a single layer on a baking sheet and roast for about 15 minutes, tossing with a spatula from time to time to be sure the vegetables roast evenly.

Just before serving, reheat the string beans in a large sauté pan drizzled with a little olive oil. Sprinkle with salt and pepper and arrange on a platter. Spoon the roasted vegetables over the string beans and serve hot or at room temperature.

Sautéed Wild Mushrooms

SERVES 4

In the autumn when mushrooms are fresh all over France, I've been known to make this as a main course and call it mushroom fricasee. Wild mushrooms are flavorful and "meaty"; they bear no relationship to our white domesticated "button" mushrooms. You'll be surprised how much flavor a good mushroom can have. This would be great with grilled veal chops or folded into an omelette.

2 pounds mixed wild mushrooms, such as cremini, shiitake, porcini, and portobello
½ cup good olive oil
1 cup chopped shallots (4 large)
4 tablespoons (½ stick) unsalted butter
2 teaspoons kosher salt
½ teaspoon freshly ground black pepper
2 tablespoons chopped garlic (6 cloves)
1 cup chopped flat-leaf parsley

Brush the caps of each mushroom with a clean sponge. Remove and discard the stems. Slice the small mushrooms thickly and cut the large ones in a large dice.

Heat the olive oil in a large (11-inch) Dutch oven or saucepan. Add the shallots and cook over low heat for 5 minutes, or until the shallots are translucent. Add the butter, mushrooms, salt, and pepper and cook over medium heat for 8 minutes, until they are tender and begin to release their juices, stirring often. Stir in the garlic and cook for 2 more minutes. Toss in the parsley, sprinkle with salt, and serve warm.

Potato Celery Root Purée

SERVES 6

I first made this dish when I took cooking classes with Lydie Marshall. I didn't even need a recipe to re-create it—after all these years, the fresh flavor is still in my mind. Don't be tempted to purée the vegetables together—a food processor makes the potatoes gummy and the food mill will leave the celery root stringy. You want this dish light and creamy.

2 pounds celery root, peeled
2 pounds Yukon gold or other boiling potatoes, peeled
2 cups milk
2 tablespoons unsalted butter
2 teaspoons kosher salt
½ teaspoon freshly ground black pepper

Cut the celery root and potatoes in very large chunks and cook them in separate pots of boiling salted water until each is very tender, about 20 minutes for the potatoes and 30 minutes for the celery root. Drain.

Meanwhile, heat the milk and butter in a small pot until scalded.

Purée the celery root with about ¾ of the hot milk in the bowl of a food processor fitted with the steel blade. Process the cooked potatoes through a food mill or potato ricer. In a large bowl, combine the puréed celery root, potatoes, salt, pepper, and enough of the remaining milk to make a firm but creamy consistency. If you're not serving immediately, keep it warm in a heat-proof bowl over simmering water. If the purée needs to sit for more than 10 minutes, add more hot milk.

Caramelized Shallots

SERVES 6

You might not usually think about serving shallots as a vegetable, but they're more flavorful and delicate than boiling onions. It's a perfect accompaniment for an everyday roast chicken, but special enough to serve on a holiday with a standing rib roast. You can peel the shallots in advance and then just give them a quick sauté and throw them into the oven before dinner.

> 6 tablespoons (¾ stick) unsalted butter
> 2 pounds fresh shallots, peeled, with roots intact
>   (see Note)
> 3 tablespoons sugar
> 3 tablespoons good red wine vinegar
> ½ teaspoon kosher salt
> ¼ teaspoon freshly ground black pepper
> 2 tablespoons chopped fresh flat-leaf parsley

Preheat the oven to 400 degrees.

Melt the butter in a 12-inch ovenproof sauté pan, add the shallots and sugar, and toss to coat. Cook over medium heat for 10 minutes, tossing occasionally, until the shallots start to brown. Add the vinegar, salt, and pepper and toss well.

Place the sauté pan in the oven and roast for 15 to 30 minutes, depending on the size of the shallots, until they are tender. Season to taste, sprinkle with parsley, and serve hot.

To peel shallots easily, drop them into a pot of boiling water for less than 1 minute. Drain, then remove the skins.

I use Cabernet Sauvignon red wine vinegar from Williams-Sonoma.

Garlic Mashed Potatoes

SERVES 6

Many of my favorite restaurants in Paris serve the vegetables family style with the main course, and mashed potatoes are always on the menu. They're usually made with lots of cream and butter, which, of course, is perfectly delicious, but sometimes they are made with olive oil, which is lighter and so much better for you. Be sure your oil is light and fruity.

I use Olio Santo olive oil from California.

½ cup garlic cloves, peeled (about 1 head)
1 cup extra-virgin olive oil
3 pounds Yukon gold potatoes, peeled and quartered
Kosher salt
1 teaspoon freshly ground black pepper
¼ cup heavy cream, half-and-half, or crème fraîche

In a small saucepan, bring the garlic and oil to a boil, then turn the heat to low and cook uncovered for 5 minutes, or until the garlic is lightly browned. Turn off the heat and set aside. The garlic will continue to cook in the oil.

Meanwhile, place the potatoes in a large pot of salted water, bring to a boil, and cook for 15 to 20 minutes, until the potatoes are very tender. With a slotted spoon, remove the potatoes from the water, reserving the cooking water, and remove the garlic from the oil, reserving the oil.

To make ahead, keep the potatoes warm in a heat-proof bowl set over the simmering water.

Process the potatoes and garlic through a food mill fitted with the medium disc. Add the reserved olive oil, 2 teaspoons of salt, the pepper, cream, and ¾ cup of the cooking water to the potatoes and mix with a wooden spoon. Add more cooking water, if necessary, until the potatoes are creamy but still firm. Season to taste and serve hot.

Herbed New Potatoes

SERVES 6

Sometimes the simplest things are the best. I love these in autumn when the potatoes are freshly dug in East Hampton and they have that good earthy flavor. You can use any small white potatoes, but if you can find Yukon gold or fingerling potatoes, they're even better.

Find potatoes that are similar in size (1½ to 2 inches diameter) so they cook in the same amount of time.

4 tablespoons (½ stick) unsalted butter
2½ pounds small white or Yukon gold potatoes, scrubbed but not peeled
2 teaspoons kosher salt
½ teaspoon freshly ground black pepper
3 tablespoons chopped mixed fresh green herbs, such as parsley, chives, and dill

Melt the butter in a Dutch oven or large heavy-bottomed pot. Add the whole potatoes, salt, and pepper and toss well. Cover the pot tightly and cook over low heat for 20 to 30 minutes, until the potatoes are just tender when tested with a small knife. From time to time, shake the pot without removing the lid to prevent the bottom potatoes from burning. Turn off the heat and allow the potatoes to steam for another 5 minutes. Don't overcook! Toss with the herbs, and serve hot.

dessert

Meringues Chantilly

Plum Raspberry Crumble

Île Flottante

Lemon Meringue Tart

Pear Clafouti

Coeur à la Crème with Raspberries

Baba au Rhum

Elephant Ears

Mango Sorbet

Ice Cream Bombe

Plum Cake "Tatin"

Chocolate Orange Mousse

Brownie Tart

Pain Perdu

Peaches in Sauternes

Coconut Madeleines

Strawberry Tarts

Profiteroles

Chocolate Truffles

Crème Brûlée

About French Cheese

One of my greatest pleasures in Paris is going to a cheese shop. I don't even have to buy anything—all I have to do is walk in and breathe the air. French cheese is very different from American cheese. First, it's often made from unpasteurized milk, so all those natural enzymes in the milk give the cheese its amazing flavor. Second, cheese in France is stored in a cool, but not refrigerated, place, so it can ripen naturally. (In the United States, we add "stabilizers" to cheese to extend its shelf life, making it rubbery. How about adding things instead that make it taste better?) Finally, in France, cheese is handled like fresh produce: It's shipped slightly under-ripe, stored for a short time until just ripe, and eaten at the peak of its flavor.

It's common here to serve cheese as an appetizer, which is too bad because I think it really fills you up before dinner. In France, cheese is instead served with a salad after the main course and before dessert. It's actually surprisingly satisfying at that point in the meal. The dinner plates are cleared, a platter of cheese and a green salad are brought out, and everyone helps themselves, family style.

Personally, I think it's almost impossible to buy really good cheeses at the peak of their flavor in a regular grocery store. Find a specialty food store or cheese shop where the owners really care about the cheese. Instead of the regular cheeses, ask for "raw milk" (unpasteurized) cheeses, if your store carries them, and taste them; believe me, the owners expect it. A perfectly fabulous Pierre Robert is flavorful and creamy at its peak but if it's under-ripe, it can be chalky and tasteless, and if over-ripe it can be pungent and ammoniated. Not exactly what you'd want to serve your dinner guests! In fact, when I was at Barefoot Contessa I loved when a customer was really interested to learn about the cheeses we carried.

But with so many options at the cheese shop, it seems difficult to know what to buy. So, how do you choose? Cheese is categorized in several ways, first by the butterfat content: low-fat has about 20 percent butterfat, and believe me, it never tastes like real cheese, so forget about it. Regular cheese such as Gruyère has 45 percent butterfat; double-cream cheeses, which are rare, have 60 percent; and triple-cream, such as Explorateur and Brillat-Savarin, have 75 percent. As you can imagine, the higher the butterfat, the creamier the cheese. There are also hard cheeses such as Comté, and soft-ripening cheeses such as Brie and Camembert. All cheeses are categorized by type of milk: While most cheeses are made from cow's milk, there are also goat's milk cheeses such as Montrachet and sheep's milk cheeses such as Prince de Claverol. Finally, there are blue cheeses, which are aged with a mold injected into them, and these are some of my favorite cheeses: Roquefort, Fourme d'Ambert, and Bleu d'Auvergne.

When I'm assembling a cheese tray, I want an assortment of flavors, textures, and shapes on the tray. For a small party, three good cheeses is just fine; for a larger one, five is even better. I serve the cheese at room temperature with a big green salad and crusty French bread or crackers. For three cheeses, I'd choose a soft-ripening cheese such as Brie, a goat cheese such as Montrachet, and a blue cheese such as Bleu d'Auvergne. For a larger tray, just add more flavors, textures, and shapes. A big clump of grapes in the middle and some green leaves on the platter always add a little style.

But once in a while there's just one cheese that's so special when it's in season that you want to serve it all by itself. Serve a spoonful of perfectly ripe Vacherin Mont d'Or on a crust of bread and your friends will go crazy. And the best part—there's no cooking!

In France, cheese is served with a salad after the main course and before dessert. It's actually satisfying at that point in the meal.

Meringues Chantilly

MAKES 12 MERINGUES

I love mastering a recipe and then making it lots of different ways. These meringue shells filled with whipped cream and berries can also become a vacherin (two large meringue discs filled with whipped cream) or big meringue cookies to serve with fruit salad.

A large pastry bag with large tips is great for piping meringues.

Don't make meringues on a humid day or they will be sticky.

Store the meringues in an airtight container at room temperature.

6 extra-large egg whites, at room temperature
¼ teaspoon cream of tartar
Kosher salt
1½ cups granulated sugar, divided
½ teaspoon pure vanilla extract
Whipped Cream (page 195)
3 pints assorted berries
Raspberry Sauce (page 190)

Preheat the oven to 200 degrees. Line 2 baking sheets with parchment paper. Using a small glass and a pencil, draw six 3½-inch circles on each piece of paper. Turn the paper face-down on the baking sheets.

In the bowl of an electric mixer fitted with the whisk attachment, beat the egg whites, cream of tartar, and a large pinch of salt on medium speed until frothy. Add 1 cup of the sugar and raise the speed to high until the egg whites form very stiff peaks. Whisk in the vanilla. Carefully fold the remaining ½ cup of sugar into the meringue. With a large star-shaped pastry tip, pipe a disc of meringue inside each circle. Pipe another layer around the edge to form the sides of the shells.

Bake for 2 hours, or until the meringues are dry and crisp but not browned. Turn off the heat and allow the meringues to sit in the oven for 4 hours or overnight.

For serving, fill each shell with whipped cream, top with berries, and serve on a puddle of raspberry sauce.

Plum Raspberry Crumble

SERVES 8

Crumbles, or what we might call crisps in America, have become quite chic in Paris. Since I'm always looking for an excuse not to roll out a pie crust, I'm very fond of these fruit desserts. This is particularly good served warm with a scoop of vanilla ice cream.

Use red plums that are firm but ripe.

2 pounds red plums, cut in half, pitted, and cut in
   1-inch wedges
⅔ cup granulated sugar, divided
1¼ cups all-purpose flour, divided
2 tablespoons orange juice
½ pint fresh raspberries
⅓ cup light brown sugar, packed
¼ teaspoon kosher salt
8 tablespoons (1 stick) cold unsalted butter, diced
½ cup quick-cooking oats
½ cup sliced almonds, plus extra for sprinkling

I use McCann's or Quaker quick-cooking oats.

Preheat the oven to 350 degrees.

In a large bowl, combine the sliced plums, ⅓ cup of the granulated sugar, ¼ cup of the flour, and the orange juice and toss well. Add the raspberries and toss lightly. Pour into a 9 × 12 × 2-inch baking dish.

For the topping, place the remaining 1 cup of flour, the remaining ⅓ cup of granulated sugar, the brown sugar, and the salt in the bowl of a food processor fitted with a steel blade and pulse a few times to combine. Add the butter and pulse until the butter is the size of peas. Pour the mixture into a bowl, add the oats, and work it with your hands until it's in large crumbles. Add ½ cup of the almonds and mix well.

Spread the topping evenly over the plums, making sure the fruit is covered. Sprinkle with some extra almonds. Bake for 40 minutes, or until the fruit is tender and bubbly and the topping is golden brown. Serve warm or at room temperature.

Île Flottante

Île flottante (floating island) is an old-fashioned French nursery dessert that will have your guests groaning with pleasure. It involves three steps, but everything except the meringue can be made a day or two ahead and then assembled just before serving. I promise you it's worth every minute it takes to make. Your friends will be licking their plates.

2½ cups sugar, divided
1½ teaspoons pure vanilla extract, divided
1½ cups (5 ounces) sliced almonds
8 extra-large egg whites, at room temperature
⅛ teaspoon kosher salt
¼ teaspoon cream of tartar
Crème Anglaise (page 191)

Preheat the oven to 350 degrees.

For the caramel, heat 1½ cups of the sugar and ½ cup water in a small, heavy-bottomed saucepan until the sugar dissolves. Cook over medium heat until the syrup turns a warm caramel color. Don't stir, just swirl it in the pan. Off the heat, add ½ cup water and ½ teaspoon of the vanilla; be careful, the syrup will bubble violently. Stir and cook over high heat until the caramel reaches 230 degrees (thread stage) on a candy thermometer. Set aside.

For the praline, combine the almonds with ¼ cup of the caramel and spread them on a sheet pan lined with parchment paper. Bake for 10 to 12 minutes, until the almonds are lightly browned. Allow to cool at room temperature and then break up in pieces.

Lower the oven to 250 degrees. Line 2 sheet pans with parchment paper.

For the meringues, beat the egg whites, salt, and cream of tartar in the bowl of an electric mixer fitted with the whisk attachment on medium speed until frothy. Turn the mixer on high speed and add the remaining 1 cup of sugar. Beat until the egg whites are very stiff and glossy. Whisk in the remaining teaspoon of vanilla. Place large mounds of meringue on the parchment paper with soup spoons and bake for 20 minutes, or until a cake tester comes out clean.

For serving, pour crème anglaise on the bottom of individual plates. Place a meringue or two on top of each serving, drizzle with caramel sauce, sprinkle with praline, and serve.

To make a day or two ahead, leave the caramel and praline at room temperature and refrigerate the crème anglaise. Bake the meringues before guests arrive and assemble the desserts just before serving.

Lemon Meringue Tart

SERVES 8

People think of lemon meringue as quintessentially American, but I see it in French pastry shops all the time. Lemon tart is certainly French, and so is meringue, so why not Lemon Meringue Tart? I have to admit that even I was impressed when this tart came out of the oven. It requires a few steps, but you can make most of it a day ahead and then bake the tart the day of the party. Your guests might not remember what you made for dinner, but they'll definitely remember dessert.

> 1¼ cups all-purpose flour
> ½ cup plus 3 tablespoons sugar
> Kosher salt
> 6 tablespoons (¾ stick) cold unsalted butter, diced
> 2 tablespoons cold Crisco
> ¼ cup ice water
> 4 extra-large egg whites, at room temperature
> ¼ teaspoon cream of tartar
> Lemon Filling (recipe follows)

Combine the flour, 3 tablespoons of the sugar, and ½ teaspoon salt in a bowl and place in the freezer for 30 minutes. Put the flour mixture in the bowl of a food processor fitted with a steel blade. Add the butter and Crisco and pulse about 10 times until the butter is in small bits. Add the ice water and process until the dough comes together. Dump on a well-floured board and form into a disc. Wrap in plastic and chill for at least 30 minutes.

Meanwhile, preheat the oven to 375 degrees.

Roll out the dough and fit into a 9-inch tart pan with removable sides. Don't stretch the dough when placing it in the pan or it will shrink during baking. Cut off the excess by rolling the pin across the top of the pan. Line the tart shell with a piece of buttered aluminum foil, butter side down, and fill it with dried beans or rice. Bake for 10 minutes. Remove the beans and foil and prick the bottom of the shell all over with a fork to allow the steam to escape. Bake for another 15 to 20 minutes, until lightly browned. Set aside to cool.

Raise the oven temperature to 425 degrees.

For the meringue, whip the egg whites, cream of tartar, and ¼ teaspoon salt in the bowl of an electric mixer fitted with the whisk attachment on high speed until frothy. With the mixer still running, slowly add the remaining ½ cup of sugar and beat until the meringue is thick and shiny, about 2 minutes.

Immediately spread the lemon filling in the cooled tart shell and pipe the meringue over it with a large star tip. Be sure the meringue covers the entire top and touches the edges of the shell, to prevent it from shrinking. Bake for 3 to 5 minutes, until the meringue is lightly browned. Cool to room temperature.

To make ahead, wrap the cooled tart shell and store at room temperature. Store the lemon filling in the refrigerator. Assemble and bake the day you plan to serve it.

LEMON FILLING

MAKES 3 CUPS

¼ pound (1 stick) unsalted butter, at room temperature
1½ cups sugar
4 extra-large eggs
3 extra-large egg yolks (save the whites for the meringue)
¼ cup finely grated lemon zest (6 to 8 lemons)
½ cup freshly squeezed lemon juice
⅛ teaspoon kosher salt

A rasp or Microplane grater zests lemons really fast.

Cream the butter and sugar in the bowl of an electric mixer fitted with the paddle attachment for 1 minute. On low speed, add the eggs and egg yolks one at a time, and then add the lemon zest, lemon juice, and salt. Don't worry; it will look curdled.

Pour the mixture into a small saucepan and cook over medium-low heat for 8 to 10 minutes, until thick, stirring constantly with a wooden spoon. Whisk briskly when it starts to thicken and cook over low heat for a minute or two, whisking constantly. Don't allow it to boil! It will be 175 degrees on an instant-read thermometer. Pour into a bowl and cool to room temperature.

Pear Clafouti

SERVES 8

Clafouti is made by pouring a pancake-like batter over fruit, so it's really easy to make. It's traditionally made with cherries, but since pears are available for more of the year, I changed the recipe. This was inspired by Debra Ponzek's book French Food, American Accent.

1 tablespoon unsalted butter, at room temperature
⅓ cup plus 1 tablespoon granulated sugar
3 extra-large eggs, at room temperature
6 tablespoons all-purpose flour
1½ cups heavy cream
2 teaspoons pure vanilla extract
1 teaspoon grated lemon zest (2 lemons)
¼ teaspoon kosher salt
2 tablespoons pear brandy, such as Poire William
2 to 3 firm but ripe Bartlett pears
Confectioners' sugar

Bartlett pears are often hard when you buy them. Allow them to sit at room temperature for a day or two until they smell ripe but are still firm.

Preheat the oven to 375 degrees. Butter a 10 × 1½-inch round baking dish and sprinkle the bottom and sides with 1 tablespoon of the granulated sugar.

Beat the eggs and the ⅓ cup of granulated sugar in the bowl of an electric mixer fitted with the paddle attachment on medium-high speed until light and fluffy, about 3 minutes. On low speed, mix in the flour, cream, vanilla extract, lemon zest, salt, and pear brandy. Set aside for 10 minutes.

Meanwhile, peel, quarter, core, and slice the pears. Arrange the slices in a single layer, slightly fanned out, in the baking dish. Pour the batter over the pears and bake until the top is golden brown and the custard is firm, 35 to 40 minutes. Serve warm or at room temperature, sprinkled with confectioners' sugar.

Coeur à la Crème
with Raspberries

SERVES 6 TO 8

This amazing dessert was inspired by my friend Anna Pump in her Loaves and Fishes Cookbook. *This is really easy to make and can be prepared days before a party. Believe me, your friends will go crazy.*

12 ounces cream cheese, at room temperature
1¼ cups confectioners' sugar
2½ cups cold heavy cream
2 teaspoons pure vanilla extract
¼ teaspoon grated lemon zest
Seeds scraped from 1 vanilla bean
Raspberry Sauce (recipe follows)
1 pint fresh raspberries

Place the cream cheese and confectioners' sugar in the bowl of an electric mixer fitted with the paddle attachment and beat on high speed for 2 minutes. Scrape down the beater and bowl with a rubber spatula and change the beater for the whisk attachment. With the mixer on low speed, add the heavy cream, vanilla, lemon zest, and vanilla seeds and beat on high speed until the mixture is very thick, like whipped cream.

Line a heart-shaped mold with cheesecloth so the ends drape over the sides and place it on a plate, making sure that there is space between the bottom of the mold and the plate for the liquid to drain. Pour the cream mixture into the cheesecloth, fold the ends over the top, and refrigerate overnight.

To serve, discard the liquid, unmold the cream onto a plate, and drizzle raspberry sauce around the base. Serve with raspberries and extra sauce.

If you double this recipe, it won't set. For a large group, make two molds.

I use a heart-shaped dish with perforations, but you can also use a 7-inch sieve, which will make a rounded crème. Suspend the sieve over a bowl to drain.

Raspberry Sauce

MAKES 2 CUPS

For a sauce, nothing is easier or fresher tasting than this raspberry sauce. It's delicious with Coeur à la Crème or Meringues Chantilly (page 176). It's also great for entertaining because you can make it a day or two in advance. Framboise is a clear raspberry eau-de-vie that you can find at the liquor store.

1 half-pint fresh raspberries
½ cup sugar
1 cup (12 ounces) seedless raspberry jam
1 tablespoon framboise liqueur

The cream and the raspberry sauce can each be made a few days ahead.

Place the raspberries, sugar, and ¼ cup water in a small saucepan. Bring to a boil, lower the heat, and simmer for 4 minutes. Pour the cooked raspberries, the jam, and framboise into the bowl of a food processor fitted with the steel blade and process until smooth. Chill.

Crème Anglaise
VANILLA SAUCE

MAKES 2 CUPS

Crème anglaise is one of the basics of French cooking. It's a vanilla dessert sauce but also becomes ice cream when it's frozen, and it evolves into a Bavarian when you add gelatin and whipped cream. Crème anglaise usually doesn't contain cornstarch, but for me, it's a little extra assurance that I won't end up with vanilla scrambled eggs.

    4 extra-large egg yolks
    ½ cup sugar
    1 teaspoon cornstarch
    1¾ cups scalded milk
    1 teaspoon pure vanilla extract
    1½ teaspoons Cognac
    Seeds of ½ vanilla bean (optional)

To scald milk, heat it to just below the boiling point.

Beat the egg yolks and sugar in the bowl of an electric mixer fitted with the paddle attachment on medium-high speed for 3 minutes, or until very thick. Reduce to low speed, and add the cornstarch.

With the mixer still on low, slowly pour the hot milk into the eggs. Pour the custard mixture into a saucepan and cook over low heat, stirring constantly with a wooden spoon, until thickened. The custard will coat the spoon like heavy cream. Don't cook it above 180 degrees or the eggs will scramble!

Pour the sauce through a fine strainer, add the vanilla extract, Cognac, and vanilla seeds, if using, and chill.

Baba au Rhum

SERVES 8

Baba au rhum was one of the first things I ever made for my husband when we were first married, and we still love it. Most babas have a strong, slightly harsh, rum bite, but I added a little vanilla to the syrup and it rounds out the flavor perfectly for me.

$\frac{1}{3}$ cup dried currants

1 tablespoon good dark rum

5 tablespoons unsalted butter, at room temperature

$\frac{1}{2}$ cup milk

1 package dry yeast

2 tablespoons sugar

2 extra-large eggs, at room temperature

$1\frac{2}{3}$ cups all-purpose flour

$\frac{1}{2}$ teaspoon kosher salt

Rum Syrup (recipe follows)

$\frac{3}{4}$ cup apricot preserves

Whipped Cream (recipe follows)

If you need eggs at room temperature in a hurry, place them in a bowl of warm water for about 5 minutes.

Combine the currants and rum in a small bowl and set aside. Melt 1 tablespoon of the butter and brush a 5-cup ($6\frac{1}{2} \times 3\frac{1}{2}$-inch) tube pan or kugelhopf mold with the melted butter. Be sure to coat every crevice of the pan. Heat the milk to 115 degrees and then pour it into the bowl of an electric mixer fitted with the paddle attachment. Stir in the yeast and sugar and allow to sit for 5 minutes.

With the mixer on low speed, first add the eggs, then the flour, salt, and remaining 4 tablespoons of butter. Raise the speed to medium-high and beat for 5 minutes. Scrape down the bowl and beater to form the dough into a ball. It will be very soft. Cover the bowl with a damp towel and allow it to rise until doubled in size, about 1 hour.

You can make the cake a day ahead but leave it wrapped at room temperature. Soak the cake the day of the party.

Drain the currants, fold them into the dough with a spatula, and spoon into the prepared pan. Smooth the top, cover the pan with a damp towel, and allow to rise until the dough reaches the top of the pan, 50 minutes to 1 hour.

Meanwhile, preheat the oven to 375 degrees and make the rum syrup.

Bake the cake for about 30 minutes, or until a toothpick comes out clean. Allow to cool for 10 minutes, then tap it out of the cake pan onto a baking rack set over a sheet pan. Pour all of the rum syrup *very* slowly onto the warm cake, allowing it all to soak in thoroughly. Amazingly, the liquid will be absorbed into the cake, so be sure to use all of the syrup.

Heat the preserves with 1 tablespoon of water until runny, press it through a sieve, and brush it on the cake. Serve with whipped cream piped into the middle of the cake plus an extra bowl on the side.

RUM SYRUP

I use Myers's Jamaican dark rum.

  1 cup sugar
  ⅔ cup good dark rum
  ½ teaspoon pure vanilla extract

Place the sugar and 1½ cups water in a small saucepan and cook over high heat until the sugar dissolves. Pour into a 4-cup heat-proof measuring cup and allow to cool. Add the rum and vanilla and set aside.

WHIPPED CREAM

MAKES 4 CUPS

2 cups (1 pint) cold heavy cream
2 tablespoons sugar
2 teaspoons pure vanilla extract

Whip the cream in the bowl of an electric mixer fitted with the whisk attachment. When it starts to thicken, add the sugar and vanilla and continue to whip until the cream forms stiff peaks. Don't overbeat, or you'll end up with butter!

Elephant Ears

PALMIERS

MAKES 40 TO 45 COOKIES

Ladurée, a historic pastry shop in Paris, makes huge palmiers that are positively addictive. I find those big ones hard to make, so I bake smaller ones to serve with ice cream. They're surprisingly simple as long as you start with pre-made puff pastry. It's best to allow the pastry to defrost overnight in the refrigerator so the dough is pliable but still very cold before you bake it.

2 cups sugar
⅛ teaspoon kosher salt
2 sheets Pepperidge Farm puff pastry, defrosted

Preheat the oven to 450 degrees.

Combine the sugar and kosher salt. Pour 1 cup of the sugar-salt mixture on a flat surface such as a wooden board or marble slab. Unfold the first sheet of puff pastry onto the sugar and pour ½ cup of the sugar mixture on top, spreading it evenly on the puff pastry. This is not about sprinkling, it's about an even covering of sugar. With a rolling pin, lightly roll the dough until it's a 13-inch square and the sugar is pressed into the puff pastry on top and bottom. Fold the sides of the square toward the center so they go halfway to the middle. Fold them again so the two folds meet exactly at the middle of the dough. Then fold one half over the other half as though closing a book. You will have 6 layers. Slice the dough into ⅜-inch slices and place the slices, cut side up, on baking sheets lined with parchment paper. Place the second sheet of pastry on the sugared board, sprinkle with the remaining ½ cup of sugar mixture, and continue as above.

(There will be quite a bit of sugar left over on the board.) Slice and arrange on baking sheets lined with parchment.

Bake the cookies for 6 minutes, or until caramelized and brown on the bottom, then turn with a spatula and bake for another 3 to 5 minutes, until caramelized on the other side. Transfer to a baking rack to cool.

To make ahead, cool completely and store in airtight plastic bags.

Mango Sorbet

MAKES 1¹/2 QUARTS; SERVES 6

There's a historic store in Paris on Île Saint-Louis called Berthillon that makes what seems like a million incredible flavors of ice cream. We had mango sorbet there that tasted just like frozen mangoes, so I had to come home and make some. Sorbet is best served right after you make it, but I found that if you freeze it, allow it to defrost a bit, then purée it in the food processor before serving, it's still creamy and delicious.

> ¾ cup sugar
> 5 large ripe mangoes, peeled and seeded
> ¼ cup freshly squeezed orange juice
> ¼ teaspoon kosher salt

Place the sugar and ½ cup water in a small saucepan and cook until the sugar dissolves. Set aside.

Place the mangoes in a food processor fitted with the steel blade and purée. You should have about 5 cups of mango. If you want a smoother sorbet, you can process the purée through a food mill fitted with a medium blade.

Combine the mango, sugar syrup, orange juice, and salt and refrigerate until cold. Freeze in an ice cream machine according to the manufacturer's directions. (The sorbet will be soft.) Serve directly from the ice cream machine.

If you want to make the sorbet ahead of time, freeze it in plastic containers. Allow it to soften in the refrigerator for 2 hours, then put it in a food processor fitted with the steel blade. Process, adding enough extra orange juice to make a smooth but frozen sorbet. Serve immediately.

Buy the mangoes a few days early to allow them to get ripe and juicy.

Ice Cream Bombe

SERVES 8

This is really a fun dessert. Form this into a mold and serve it with a cookie on the side. If you don't have time to prepare the mango sorbet, Häagen-Dazs makes a good one, and believe me, your friends will have just as much fun. The good news is that you can make this ahead of time. I serve it with fresh raspberries and raspberry sauce (page 190).

2 pints Mango Sorbet (page 199) or 2 pints store-bought mango sorbet, softened
1½ pints good raspberry sorbet, softened
1 pint good strawberry ice cream, softened

I prefer Häagen-Dazs ice creams and sorbets.

Freeze an 8-inch bowl. When it's cold, place the mango sorbet in the bowl and press it against the sides of the bowl. If you have a 6½-inch bowl the same shape as the 8-inch bowl (such as from a set of nesting bowls), press it into the sorbet to make the layer even. Remove the smaller bowl and freeze for 30 minutes.

Williams-Sonoma has a terrific set of glass nesting bowls that are useful for this recipe.

Spread an even layer of softened raspberry sorbet on top of the mango sorbet (a 4½-inch nesting bowl helps with this) and freeze for another 30 minutes. Finally, spoon in enough softened strawberry ice cream to fill the bowl. Freeze until hard.

To soften sorbets, put them in the microwave just until they're spreadable.

To unmold, dip the bowl up to the rim in warm water. Run a knife around the edge to loosen the bombe and unmold upside down onto a flat plate. You may need to run a flexible metal spatula along the edge of the bombe to release it. Freeze until ready to serve. Serve in wedges.

Plum Cake "Tatin"

SERVES 6

When we're in Paris, Jeffrey and I love to have dinner at home and then walk down to Café de Flore for Tarte Tatin for dessert. This cake takes its idea from that French classic, which is made with apples, but this is so much easier. If plums are out of season, I make it with two ripe Bartlett pears, peeled and cut into wedges. While it's perfectly delicious on its own, it's even better with a dollop of Whipped Cream (page 195) or crème fraîche.

6 tablespoons (¾ stick) unsalted butter, at room
    temperature, plus extra for greasing the dish
10 to 12 purple "prune" plums, cut in half and pitted
1¾ cups granulated sugar, divided
2 extra-large eggs, at room temperature
⅓ cup sour cream
½ teaspoon grated lemon zest
½ teaspoon pure vanilla extract
1 cup plus 2 tablespoons all-purpose flour
½ teaspoon baking powder
¼ teaspoon kosher salt
Confectioners' sugar

Prune plums are the blue ones available in late August and early autumn. Sometimes they're called Italian plums.

Preheat the oven to 350 degrees. Generously butter a 9-inch glass pie dish and arrange the plums in the dish, cut side down.

Combine 1 cup of the granulated sugar and ⅓ cup water in a small saucepan and cook over high heat until it turns a warm amber color, about 360 degrees on a candy thermometer. Swirl the pan but don't stir. Pour evenly over the plums.

Meanwhile, cream the 6 tablespoons of butter and the remaining ¾ cup of granulated sugar in the bowl of an electric mixer fitted with the paddle attachment, until light and fluffy. Lower the speed and beat in the eggs one at a time. Add the sour cream, zest, and vanilla and mix until combined. Sift together the flour, baking powder, and salt and, with the mixer on low speed, add it to the butter mixture. Mix only until combined.

Pour the cake batter evenly over the plums and bake for 30 to 40 minutes, until a cake tester comes out clean. Cool for 15 minutes, then invert the cake onto a flat plate. If a plum sticks, ease it out and replace it in the design on top of the cake. Serve warm or at room temperature, dusted with confectioners' sugar.

Chocolate Orange Mousse

SERVES 6 TO 8

In Paris when you order chocolate mousse at a bistro, you're sometimes offered a big communal bowl from which to serve yourself. When my husband, Jeffrey, went to a bistro on his own he thought the bowl of chocolate mousse was all for him. Boy, were they surprised—and was he sorry!

6 ounces good semisweet chocolate, chopped
2 ounces good bittersweet chocolate, chopped
¼ cup Grand Marnier liqueur
1 teaspoon pure vanilla extract
1 teaspoon grated orange zest
12 tablespoons (1½ sticks) unsalted butter, at room temperature
8 extra-large eggs, at room temperature, separated
½ cup plus 2 tablespoons sugar
Pinch of kosher salt
½ cup cold heavy cream
Whipped Cream (page 195), for decoration
Mandarin oranges, drained, for decoration

It's easier to separate cold eggs, but egg whites at room temperature whip better.

Be sure the chocolate and butter are really at room temperature before you combine them.

Combine the two chocolates, Grand Marnier, ¼ cup water, and the vanilla in a heat-proof bowl. Set it over a pan of simmering water just until the chocolate melts. Cool completely to room temperature. Whisk in the orange zest and butter until combined.

Place the egg yolks and ½ cup of the sugar in the bowl of an electric mixer fitted with the paddle attachment. Beat on high speed for 4 minutes, or until very thick and pale yellow. With the mixer on low speed, add the chocolate mixture. Transfer to a large bowl.

Place 1 cup of egg whites (save or discard the rest), the salt, and 1 tablespoon of the sugar in the bowl of an electric mixer fitted with the whisk attachment. Beat on high speed until firm but not dry. Whisk half of the egg whites into the chocolate mixture; then fold the rest in carefully with a rubber spatula.

Without cleaning the bowl or whisk, whip the heavy cream and the remaining tablespoon of sugar until firm. Fold the whipped cream into the chocolate mixture. Pour the mousse into individual dishes or an 8-cup serving bowl. Chill and decorate with whipped cream and oranges. Serve with extra whipped cream on the side.

This can be made to serve family style (page 170) or as individual servings. To make one large mousse, a soufflé dish 3¼ inches high and 7½ inches in diameter is the perfect size.

Brownie Tart

SERVES 8

*At Barefoot Contessa, we made what seemed like millions of brownie
pies over twenty-five years. Sometimes I feel like making a familiar dish
with a bit of French elegance, so I decided to bake this very American
pie in a French tart pan. Voilà! It's an elegant French dessert. A puddle
of crème anglaise on the plate doesn't hurt, either.*

I use Hershey's
semisweet choco-
late chips.

6 tablespoons (¾ stick) unsalted butter
3¼ cups (20 ounces) semisweet chocolate chips
3 extra-large eggs
1 cup sugar
1 tablespoon instant coffee granules
½ teaspoon pure vanilla extract
½ cup all-purpose flour
¼ teaspoon baking powder
¼ teaspoon kosher salt
1 cup (4 ounces) chopped walnuts
2 tablespoons heavy cream
Crème Anglaise (page 191)

Preheat the oven to 350 degrees. Grease and flour an 11-inch
tart pan with removable sides.

Melt the butter in a bowl set over simmering water. Add 2 cups
of the chocolate chips, remove from the heat, and stir until the
chocolate melts. Set aside to cool completely.

In the bowl of an electric mixer fitted with the paddle attachment, beat the eggs, sugar, coffee, and vanilla on medium-high
speed until light and fluffy, about 3 minutes. Stir in the cooled
chocolate. In a medium bowl, combine the flour, baking powder,
salt, 1 cup of the chocolate chips, and the walnuts. Fold the flour

mixture into the batter until just combined. Pour into the pan and bake for 35 to 40 minutes, until the center is puffed (the top may crack). The inside will still be very soft. Cool to room temperature before removing the sides of the tart pan.

Melt the remaining ¼ cup of chocolate chips with the heavy cream and drizzle on the tart. Serve in wedges alone or on a puddle of crème anglaise.

Tart pans come in all different sizes, and manufacturers measure them differently. I measure the top from rim to rim.

Pain Perdu

SERVES 6

French toast for dessert? Who wouldn't love that? This is easy to make but best for a small party, since you have to get up between dinner and dessert to cook it. If you're eating in the kitchen and your friends like to cook with you, this old-fashioned French nursery dessert is really worth the effort. Your guests will love you.

½ pint fresh strawberries, hulled and sliced
2 tablespoons sugar, divided
3 tablespoons Grand Marnier, divided
6 extra-large eggs
1½ cups milk or half-and-half
2 tablespoons honey
1½ teaspoons pure vanilla extract
1 teaspoon grated orange zest
2 teaspoons kosher salt
1 large brioche loaf (page 92) or challah
Unsalted butter
Vegetable oil
½ cup (1½ ounces) sliced blanched almonds, toasted
Confectioners' sugar, to serve

To toast almonds, place them in a dry sauté pan and cook over low heat for 5 to 10 minutes, tossing frequently, until lightly browned.

Combine the sliced strawberries, 1 tablespoon of the sugar, and 1 tablespoon of the Grand Marnier in a small bowl and set aside. Preheat the oven to 250 degrees.

In a large bowl, whisk together the eggs, milk, honey, 1 tablespoon of sugar, 2 tablespoons of Grand Marnier, the vanilla, orange zest, and salt. Slice the bread in ¾-inch slices. Pour the egg mixture into a large shallow plate and soak a few slices of bread for 4 minutes, turning once.

Heat 1 tablespoon each of butter and oil in a very large sauté pan over medium heat. Take each slice of bread from the egg mixture, dip one side in the toasted almonds, and place in the sauté pan, almond side down. (While you're cooking each batch, add more bread to the egg mixture to soak.) Cook for 2 to 3 minutes on each side, until nicely browned. Place the cooked bread on a baking sheet and keep it warm in the oven. Wipe out the pan with a dry paper towel, add more butter and oil, and continue to fry the remaining soaked bread until they're all cooked. Sprinkle with confectioners' sugar and serve hot with the strawberries.

Peaches in Sauternes

SERVES 4 TO 6

There's something about this dessert that I love; it's not as dramatic as a fruit tart, but the synergy of the two ingredients is, for me, the essence of simple French food. The peaches make the Sauternes taste better and the Sauternes makes the peaches taste better. I make this in the summer when I can get luscious ripe peaches at The Milk Pail nearby in Water Mill, Long Island.

6 to 8 very ripe yellow or white peaches
3 tablespoons sugar
1 (375-ml) bottle of good Sauternes
1 tablespoon Grand Marnier

Bring a pot of water to a boil and immerse the peaches in the water for 1 to 2 minutes, until the skins are loose. Remove the peaches with a slotted spoon and place them in a bowl of cold water to stop the cooking. Peel the peaches and then slice them off the pit in wedges into a bowl. Stir in the sugar, Sauternes, and Grand Marnier. Cover and refrigerate for at least 2 hours, or overnight. Serve cool but not cold.

Coconut Madeleines

MAKES 24 MADELEINES

Generally, I avoid recipes that require a special piece of equipment, but madeleines are so special that I make an exception. They're rich little pound cakes in the form of a shell, and Marcel Proust famously reminisced about dipping them into his tea as a child. Unfortunately, these taste best right out of the oven; but if they dry out, you can always dip them in your tea.

1½ tablespoons melted butter, to grease the pans
3 extra-large eggs, at room temperature
⅔ cup sugar
1 teaspoon pure vanilla extract
¼ pound (1 stick) unsalted butter, melted and cooled
1 cup all-purpose flour
¼ cup cornstarch
½ teaspoon baking powder
¼ teaspoon kosher salt
⅓ cup sweetened shredded coconut
Confectioners' sugar (optional)

A pastry brush works best for greasing the pans.

Preheat the oven to 375 degrees. Thoroughly grease and flour the madeleine pans.

In the bowl of an electric mixer fitted with the paddle attachment, beat the eggs, sugar, and vanilla on medium speed for 3 minutes, or until light yellow and fluffy. Add the butter and mix. Sift together the flour, cornstarch, baking powder, and salt, and stir into the batter with a rubber spatula. Stir in the coconut.

With a soup spoon, drop the batter into the pans, filling each shell almost full. Bake the madeleines for 10 to 12 minutes, until they spring back when pressed. Tap the madeleines out onto a baking pan lined with parchment paper and allow to cool. Dust with confectioners' sugar, if desired.

Strawberry Tarts

MAKES 4 TARTS

When you order pastry for dessert at a French restaurant, they often bring you a whole tray to choose from. I heard about one disoriented tourist who thought the whole tray was for him—and such a good value for five francs! He ate as many as he could and then suggested that the waiter pass the rest of the tray around the restaurant because he couldn't possibly finish them all himself.

1¼ cups all-purpose flour
3 tablespoons sugar
½ teaspoon kosher salt
6 tablespoons (¾ stick) cold unsalted butter, diced
2 tablespoons cold Crisco
¼ cup ice water
2 cups Pastry Cream (page 217)
2 pints whole strawberries, hulled and halved
⅓ cup apricot jelly (see Note)
3 tablespoons shelled pistachios, halved (optional)

If you can't find apricot jelly, heat 8 ounces of apricot jam with 1 teaspoon of water and push it through a sieve.

Combine the flour, sugar, and salt in a small bowl and place in the freezer for 30 minutes. Put the flour mixture in the bowl of a food processor fitted with a steel blade. Add the butter and Crisco and pulse about 10 times, or until the butter is in the size of peas. Add the ice water and process until the dough comes together. Dump on a well-floured board and form into a disc. Wrap in plastic and chill for at least 30 minutes.

Meanwhile, preheat the oven to 375 degrees.

Roll out the dough and fit into four 4½-inch tart pans with removable sides. Don't stretch the dough when placing it in the pans or it will shrink during baking. Cut off the excess by rolling the pin across the top of each pan. Line the tart shells with a piece of buttered aluminum foil, butter side down, and fill them with dried beans or rice. Bake for 10 minutes. Remove the beans and foil, prick the bottom of the shells all over with a fork, and bake for another 15 to 20 minutes until lightly browned. Set aside to cool.

Before serving, fill the tart shells with the pastry cream. Arrange the berries decoratively on top of the cream. Melt the apricot jelly with 1 teaspoon of water and brush the top of the tarts. Sprinkle with pistachios, if using, and serve.

Pastry Cream

Making crème anglaise, a French vanilla sauce, is a delicate process because you can overcook it and end up with vanilla scrambled eggs. Pastry cream, on the other hand, has similar ingredients, but it's more like a custard. You can actually boil it without having the eggs scramble. Use it to fill fruit tarts and cream puffs.

5 extra-large egg yolks, at room temperature
¾ cup sugar
3 tablespoons cornstarch
1½ cups scalded milk
½ teaspoon pure vanilla extract
1 teaspoon Cognac
1 tablespoon unsalted butter
1 tablespoon heavy cream

To scald milk, heat it to just below the boiling point.

In the bowl of an electric mixer fitted with the paddle attachment, beat the egg yolks and sugar on medium-high speed for 4 minutes, or until very thick. Reduce to low speed, and add the cornstarch.

With the mixer still on low, slowly pour the hot milk into the egg mixture. Pour the mixture into a medium saucepan and cook over low heat, stirring constantly with a wooden spoon, until the mixture thickens, 5 to 7 minutes. Don't be alarmed when the custard comes to a boil and appears to curdle; switch to a whisk and beat vigorously. Cook, whisking constantly, for another 2 minutes; the custard will come together and become very thick, like pudding. Stir in the vanilla, Cognac, butter, and heavy cream. Pour the custard through a sieve into a bowl. Place plastic wrap directly on the custard and refrigerate until cold.

Profiteroles

*One of my favorite restaurants in Paris, Benoit, offers a few little pro-
fiteroles at the table to snack on while you're deciding about dessert!
French puff pastry, or pâte à choux, seems complicated, but once you get
the hang of it, it's pretty fast to make. Then you also can make cheese
puffs, cream puffs, and eclairs, all with the same basic recipe. Personally,
I love the combination of pastry, ice cream, and chocolate, so profiteroles
are my first choice.*

> 1 cup milk
> ¼ pound (1 stick) unsalted butter
> Pinch of kosher salt
> 1 cup all-purpose flour
> 4 extra-large eggs
> ½ cup heavy cream
> 12 ounces semisweet chocolate chips
> 2 tablespoons honey
> 2 tablespoons prepared coffee
> Good vanilla ice cream, such as Häagen-Dazs, for serving

*I use Hershey's
chocolate chips.*

Preheat the oven to 425 degrees.

Heat the milk, butter, and salt over medium heat until scalded.
When the butter is melted, add the flour all at once and beat it
with a wooden spoon until the mixture comes together and
forms a dough. Cook, stirring constantly, over low heat for
2 minutes. The flour will begin to coat the bottom of the pan.
Dump the hot mixture into the bowl of a food processor fitted
with the steel blade. Add the eggs and pulse until the eggs are
incorporated into the dough and the mixture is thick.

Spoon the mixture into a pastry bag fitted with a large plain round tip. Pipe in mounds 1½ inches wide and 1 inch high onto a baking sheet lined with parchment paper. You should have about 18 puffs. With a wet finger, lightly press down the swirl at the top of each puff. (You can also use two spoons to scoop out the mixture and shape the puffs with damp fingers.) Bake for 20 minutes, or until lightly browned, then turn off the oven and allow them to sit for another 10 minutes, until they sound hollow when tapped on the bottom. Make a small slit in the side of each puff to allow the steam to escape. Set aside to cool.

For the chocolate sauce, place the cream and chocolate chips in a bowl set over simmering water and stir just until the chocolate melts. Add the honey and coffee and stir until smooth. Set aside.

For serving, cut each profiterole in half crosswise, fill with a small scoop of ice cream, replace the top, and drizzle with slightly warm chocolate sauce.

Freeze the baked puffs in a plastic bag and reheat in a 350 degree oven for 5 to 10 minutes, until crisp. Cool before filling.

To make cream puffs, pipe with pastry cream (page 217).

Chocolate Truffles

MAKES 20 TRUFFLES

These chocolates are called truffles because they look like those wild mushrooms that are dug up by pigs. They're incredibly expensive when you buy them from a chocolate shop but not very complicated to make. You can serve them directly from the refrigerator or soft at room temperature.

3½ ounces good bittersweet chocolate
3½ ounces good semisweet chocolate
½ cup heavy cream
1½ tablespoons Grand Marnier liqueur
1 tablespoon prepared coffee
½ teaspoon good vanilla extract
Cocoa powder
Confectioners' sugar

Chop the chocolates finely and place in a bowl.

Heat the cream in a small saucepan until it boils. Immediately pour the hot cream through a fine-meshed sieve into the bowl with the chocolates. With a wire whisk, slowly stir the cream and chocolates together until the chocolate is completely melted. (If the chocolate doesn't melt completely, place the bowl over a pan of simmering water and stir for a few minutes *just* until it melts.) Whisk in the Grand Marnier, coffee, and vanilla. Cover and chill for 45 minutes to an hour until pliable but firm enough to scoop.

With two teaspoons or a 1¼-inch ice cream scoop, make dollops of the chocolate mixture and place on a baking sheet lined with parchment paper. Refrigerate for about 15 minutes, until firm enough to roll into rough spheres. Roll in cocoa powder and chill. Truffles are best when they're allowed to set overnight in the refrigerator. Roll in confectioners' sugar and serve chilled or at room temperature.

There are many good chocolates, such as Lindt, Valrhona, and Callebaut.

Semisweet chocolate chips may contain stabilizers or flour gluten, which gives them a different consistency from chocolate bars.

Crème Brûlée

SERVES 5 TO 6

Crème brûlée is the ultimate "guy" dessert. Make it and he'll follow you anywhere. Most recipes are a little more complicated, but this one you can make in about ten minutes—and it's really good. Caramelizing the top adds the "Wow!" factor.

1 extra-large egg
4 extra-large egg yolks
½ cup sugar, plus 1 tablespoon for each serving
3 cups heavy cream
1 teaspoon pure vanilla extract
1 tablespoon Grand Marnier

If there's foam on the mixture, skim it off with a spoon before pouring it into the ramekins.

A kitchen blowtorch isn't as scary as it sounds, and it's much better than the broiler.

The custards can be made up to 3 days in advance; caramelize the tops before serving.

Preheat the oven to 300 degrees.

In the bowl of an electric mixer fitted with the paddle attachment, mix the egg, egg yolks, and ½ cup of the sugar together on low speed until just combined. Meanwhile, scald the cream in a small saucepan until it's very hot to the touch but not boiled. With the mixer on low speed, slowly add the cream to the eggs. Add the vanilla and Grand Marnier and pour into 6- to 8-ounce ramekins until almost full.

Place the ramekins in a baking pan and carefully pour boiling water into the pan to come halfway up the sides of the ramekins. Bake for 35 to 40 minutes, until the custards are set when gently shaken. Remove the custards from the water bath, cool to room temperature, and refrigerate until firm.

To serve, spread 1 tablespoon of sugar evenly on the top of each ramekin and heat with a kitchen blowtorch until the sugar caramelizes evenly. Allow to sit at room temperature for a minute until the caramelized sugar hardens.

resources

Celery root

Haricots verts

Morels

Puff pastry

French Ingredients you'll want to try

Green lentils

Endive

Fennel

Sea salt

FLEUR DE SEL DE CAMARGUE

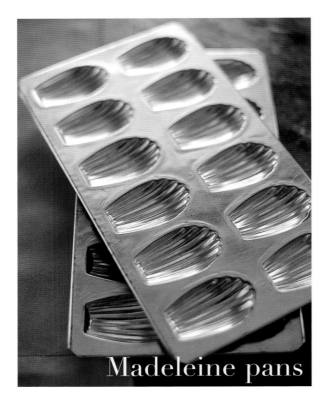

Madeleine pans

La coeur

Soufflé dish

Crème brûlée dishes

French Cookware you'll want to have

Mouli food mill

Pastry bag
with large tips

Mandoline

Tart pans with
removable sides

If You're Going . . .

There are so many wonderful restaurants, specialty food stores, and cookware emporiums in Paris that it's impossible for me to compile a complete directory. However, for anyone going to Paris, I thought I would compile a list of my favorite places—the ones I visit over and over again. If you are *really* interested in food, the most indispensable resource is Patricia Wells's book *The Food Lover's Guide to Paris*. I don't leave home without it.

SPECIALTY FOODS

La Grande Epicerie de Paris
At Bon Marché
38, rue de Sèvres
7th arrondissement
This store has everything you could possibly want in a specialty food store, and I mean *everything*!

Boulevard Raspail Street Market
Boulevard Raspail from rue du Cherche-Midi to rue de Rennes
6th arrondissement
Tuesdays, Fridays, and Sundays
It was this market that made me want to live in Paris. Bakers sell their own homemade breads and farmers have tables with their precious home-grown raspberries. Don't miss the potato pancakes and the rotisserie chickens cooking at the entrance on rue du Cherche-Midi.

Gérard Mulot
76, rue de Seine
6th arrondissement
This is an exquisite international take-out shop. Order salmon and foie gras for a party or get a sandwich and a pastry and go down the block to eat it in the Luxembourg Gardens. It's all delicious.

Hédiard
21, place de la Madeleine
8th arrondissement
and other locations
This is old-world French food, from exotic fruit to wonderful spices from India. Their boxed cheese straws are perfect to serve with a glass of Champagne.

Mariage Frères
30, rue du Bourg-Tibourg
4th arrondissement
and other locations
If you like tea, make a pilgrimage here. Since 1854 they've been selling the most amazing teas (my favorites are Marco Polo and French Breakfast) plus tea pots, cups, and tea paraphernalia. You can also stay for a delicious pick-me-up in their beautiful tearoom.

Poilâne

BREAD

Poilâne
8, rue du Cherche-Midi
6th arrondissement
This is considered to be the best bread in Paris. Although Lionel Poilâne and his wife died tragically in a plane crash in 2002, their daughter Apollonia carries on the family tradition. Don't miss this shop; it's my favorite place in Paris. The good news is they will FedEx their famous four-pound loaf to your door here for only $35, including shipping (www.Poilane.com).

Keyser

8, rue Monge
5th arrondissement
Everyone wonders if Eric
Keyser is the next Poilâne.
You don't have to wonder;
they're both extraordinary. I
love the bread called a flute, a
type of baguette that has lots
of flavor.

Poujauran

20, rue Jean Nicot
7th arrondissement
Jean-Luc Poujauran claims to
have produced the first
baguette from organically
grown wheat, and it's also one
of the best in Paris. He also
makes lots of other delicious
cakes and pastries.

Place Furstenberg

Poilâne

CHEESE

Barthélémy

51, rue de Grenelle
7th arrondissement
Just walk in and breathe the
air. You'll know that you're in
Paris because cheese here is so
different from cheese in the
United States. I love this store.
Ask for tastes; the service is as
good as the cheeses.

Quatrehomme

62, rue de Sèvres
7th arrondissement
My friends who know cheese
are crazy about this shop. The
selection is truly unbelievable.

PASTRIES AND CHOCOLATE

Ladurée

16, rue Royale
8th arrondissement, or
21, rue Bonaparte
6th arrondissement
and other locations
One of the oldest and most
elegant tea salons and pastry
shops in Paris; very famous for
its delicious macaroons.

Pierre Hermé

72, rue Bonaparte
at place Saint-Sulpice
6th arrondissement
Very beautiful and modern
pastries with unusual flavor
combinations such as peach,
apricot, and saffron; passion
fruit and milk chocolate; and
pistachio and white chocolate.

Dalloyau

101, rue du Faubourg
Saint-Honoré
8th arrondissement and
other locations
Very elegant and traditional
French pastry shop filled with
wonderful pastries and
chocolates.

Berthillon

31, rue Saint-Louis-en-l'Isle
4th arrondissement
(Île Saint-Louis)
There is no ice cream in the
world like Berthillon's. The
mango ice cream tastes like
frozen mangoes and the
chocolate ice cream like frozen
truffles. I particularly admire
the fact that—in true French
fashion—although it's an ice
cream store, it's closed in
August!

La Maison du Chocolat
225, rue du Faubourg
Saint-Honoré
8th arrondissement
19, rue de Sèvres
6th arrondissement
and other locations
Considered by many to be the
finest chocolates in Paris. I
also love the traditionally
flavored macaroons.

Legrand

WINE

Legrand Fille et Fils
1, rue de la Banque
2nd arrondissement
This is the quintessential old
Paris wine store; it's well
stocked and not the least bit
pretentious. After browsing
through their extraordinary
choice of wines, go out the
back door through the
beautiful glass-enclosed
courtyard and check out their
shop filled with wine glasses
and accessories. The café is
also wonderful.

La Dernière Goutte
6, rue Bourbon-le-Château
6th arrondissement
American owner Juan Sanchez
runs this jewel of a store with

E. Dehillerin

an amazing selection of wines
from all the regions of France.

COOKWARE

E. Dehillerin
18 and 20, rue Coquillière
1st arrondissement
This is the IT of cookware. I
dream about going to this
place. They have every piece
of professional French
cookware imaginable and the
nicest staff to help you. I
promise you'll be inspired.

TABLEWARE

Muriel Grateau
37, rue de Beaune
7th arrondissement
Madame Grateau designs the
most amazing lines of dishes,
glassware, and linens
imaginable. She's resisted the
temptation to sell them
internationally, so you have to
visit the mecca in Paris. Her
tableware is simple enough to
use every day but so elegant
you'll want it for company.

Doucement
18, avenue Montaigne
8th arrondissement
This is my favorite place in
Paris for table linens. Marie
will embroider the design you
choose on a tablecloth and
napkins. It's expensive, but if
you take care of the linens,
they'll last a lifetime.

The Conran Shop
117, rue du Bac
7th arrondissement
Modern, well-designed
housewares from London.

Catherine Memmi
32–34, rue Saint-Sulpice
6th arrondissement
Simple, modern tableware in
beautiful neutral colors.

Flamant
8, rue Furstenberg
6th arrondissement
Simple and stylish tableware
from Belgium. They also
have a good small flower
shop next door.

Muriel Grateau

Marianne Robic

FLOWERS

Marianne Robic
39, rue de Babylone
7th arrondissement
I was devastated when
Marianne closed her store on
rue de Bourgogne, but now
she's reopened a larger shop
on rue de Babylone and it has
all of her fabulous style. As a
friend of mine says, "You
don't choose the flowers here,
they choose you." I always buy
much more than I expected.
There are gorgeous flowers,
branches, seed pods, and vases
that will change your idea of
flower arrangements. Don't
miss this.

Christian Tortu
6, carrefour de l'Odéon
6th arrondissement
Christian Tortu turned the
style world upside down a
decade ago with his dramatic
modern designs such as
all-white and all-green
arrangements. Lately, his
designs have become a little
too modern for my taste, but
I still have to go by and see
what he's doing.

Une Pensée Fleuriste
26, rue de l'Université
7th arrondissement
These young florists do the
most surprising and beautiful
seasonal arrangements with
branches of berries and
interesting seed pods mixed
with gorgeous flowers.

RESTAURANTS

Chez L'Ami Louis
32, rue du Vertbois
3rd arrondissement
Although the prices are
outrageous, the food here is
beyond delicious. As Patricia
Wells says, "people beg, cry,
weep for a table." For a special
occasion, we always have the
best dinner and the most fun
here.

Benoit
20, rue Saint-Martin
4th arrondissement
This is the quintessential old
Paris bistro. It was founded
here in 1914 yet the food and
service are still outstanding.
Save room for the coffee
vacherin with prunes in
Armagnac for dessert.

Le Duc
243, boulevard Raspail
14th arrondissement
This is one of my favorite fish
restaurants in Paris; the room
feels like a cozy dining room
and the fish is simply and
elegantly prepared. It's the
essence of a chic Parisian
restaurant.

Chez Georges
1, rue du Mail
2nd arrondissement
This is delicious traditional
French food in an old-
fashioned setting. If you're in
the mood for herring and
potatoes, beef bourguignon,
and baba au rhum, this is
your place.

Marco Polo
8, rue de Condé
at rue Saint-Sulpice
6th arrondissement
When you've been to all the
French restaurants and feel
like a change, sit at one of the
tables on the terrace of this
wonderful neighborhood
restaurant and savor the
tomato, mozzarella di buffala,
and basil salad plus a big
steaming plate of delicious
pasta pesto. Albano will take
very good care of you.

Flamant

Credits

Unless otherwise indicated, tableware shown in the photographs is privately owned.

page 1: china and glassware from Muriel Grateau
    37, rue de Beaune
    Paris 75007, France
    011 33 1 40 20 42 82

page 16: china, glassware, and linens from Muriel Grateau

page 18: glass and china from Crate & Barrel
    800-323-5461

page 28: wineglass from Sentimento
    306 East 61st Street
    New York, NY 10021
    212-750-3111

page 37: placemat from Hermès
    691 Madison Avenue
    New York, NY 10022
    212-751-3181

page 51: soufflé dish from Williams-Sonoma
    800-541-2233

pages 78 and 79: most flowers by Marianne Robic
    39, rue de Babylone
    Paris 75007, France
    011 33 1 53 63 14 00

page 80: china from Muriel Grateau

page 86: glass from Sentimento,
    napkin from Hermès,
    platter from Wisteria Catalog
    www.wisteria.com
    800-320-9757

page 96: plate from Barneys New York
    660 Madison Avenue
    New York, NY 10021
    212-826-8900

page 98: plate from Lucca & Co.
    67 Gansevoort Street
    New York, NY 10014
    212-741-0400

page 103: photograph by Richard Avedon

page 125: plate from Lucca & Co.

page 155: All Clad sauté pan from Williams-Sonoma

page 157: napkin from Muriel Grateau

page 161: placemat from Hermès

page 167: bowl from Barneys New York

page 179: white baking dish from Williams-Sonoma

page 189: heart-shaped mold from Bridge Kitchenware
    214 East 52nd Street
    New York, NY 10022
    212-688-4220

page 193: platter from Wisteria Catalog

page 201: placemat from Hermès

page 209: placemat and napkins from Hermès

page 210: napkin from Hermès

page 223: crème brûlée dishes from Williams-Sonoma

Index

Conversion Chart
Equivalent Imperial and Metric Measurements

American cooks use standard containers, the 8-ounce cup and a tablespoon that takes exactly 16 level fillings to fill that cup level. Measuring by cup makes it very difficult to give weight equivalents, as a cup of densely packed butter will weigh considerably more than a cup of flour. The easiest way therefore to deal with cup measurements in recipes is to take the amount by volume rather than by weight. Thus the equation reads:

1 cup = 240 ml = 8 fl. oz.   ½ cup = 120 ml = 4 fl. oz.

It is possible to buy a set of American cup measures in major stores around the world.

In the States, butter is often measured in sticks. One stick is the equivalent of 8 tablespoons. One tablespoon of butter is therefore the equivalent to ½ ounce/15 grams.

LIQUID MEASURES

Fluid Ounces	U.S.	Imperial	Milliliters
	1 teaspoon	1 teaspoon	5
¼	2 teaspoons	1 dessertspoon	10
½	1 tablespoon	1 tablespoon	14
1	2 tablespoons	2 tablespoons	28
2	¼ cup	4 tablespoons	56
4	½ cup		110
5		¼ pint or 1 gill	140
6	¾ cup		170
8	1 cup		225
9			250, ¼ liter
10	1¼ cups	½ pint	280
12	1½ cups		340
15		¾ pint	420
16	2 cups		450
18	2¼ cups		500, ½ liter
20	2½ cups	1 pint	560
24	3 cups		675
25		1¼ pints	700
27	3½ cups		750
30	3¾ cups	1½ pints	840
32	4 cups or 1 quart		900
35		1¾ pints	980
36	4½ cups		1000, 1 liter
40	5 cups	2 pints or 1 quart	1120

SOLID MEASURES

U.S. and Imperial Measures		Metric Measures	
Ounces	Pounds	Grams	Kilos
1		28	
2		56	
3½		100	
4	¼	112	
5		140	
6		168	
8	½	225	
9		250	¼
12	¾	340	
16	1	450	
18		500	½
20	1¼	560	
24	1½	675	
27		750	¾
28	1¾	780	
32	2	900	
36	2¼	1000	1
40	2½	1100	
48	3	1350	
54		1500	1½

OVEN TEMPERATURE EQUIVALENTS

Fahrenheit	Celsius	Gas Mark	Description
225	110	¼	Cool
250	130	½	
275	140	1	Very Slow
300	150	2	
325	170	3	Slow
350	180	4	Moderate
375	190	5	
400	200	6	Moderately Hot
425	220	7	Fairly Hot
450	230	8	Hot
475	240	9	Very Hot
500	250	10	Extremely Hot

Any broiling recipes can be used with the grill of the oven, but beware of high-temperature grills.

EQUIVALENTS FOR INGREDIENTS

all-purpose flour—plain flour
coarse salt—kitchen salt
cornstarch—cornflour
eggplant—aubergine

half and half—12% fat milk
heavy cream—double cream
light cream—single cream
lima beans—broad beans

scallion—spring onion
unbleached flour—strong, white flour
zest—rind
zucchini—courgettes or marrow

Recipe Index

For menus, please visit BarefootContessa.com